Have an Out-of-Body Experience in 30 Days

Also by Keith Harary and Pamela Weintraub

The 30-Day Altered States Series
Lucid Dreams in 30 Days: The Creative Sleep Program
Right Brain Learning in 30 Days:
The Whole Mind Program
Memory Enhancement in 30 Days:
The Total Recall Program
Mystical Experiences in 30 Days:
The Higher Consciousness Program
Inner Sex in 30 Days: The Erotic Fulfillment Program

Also by Keith Harary

Who Do You Think You Are? Explore Your Many-Sided Self
with the Berkeley Personality Profile

Also by Pamela Weintraub

Nurturing the Unborn Child: A Nine-Month Program for Soothing,
Stimulating, and Communicating with Your Baby
The Complete Idiot's Guide to Surviving Divorce
You Can Save the Animals: 50 Things to Do Right Now
The Omni Interviews
Medical Emergency!: The St. Luke's-Roosevelt Hospital Center
Book of Emergency Medicine

Have an Out-of-Body Experience in 30 Days

The Free Flight Program

Keith Harary, Ph.D.,
and
Pamela Weintraub

St. Martin's Griffin New York

For James Kidd, who made the research possible.

ISBN 0-312-19983-X

First St. Martin's Griffin Edition: March 1999

10 9 8 7 6 5 4 3 2 1

CONTENTS

INTRODUCTION

It may feel as familiar as falling out of bed, or as startling as waking up floating near the ceiling in the middle of the night. It could happen spontaneously while you're relaxing in your favorite chair listening to music, or as you await medics following a highway crash. Defined by the sensation that your mind and your body exist in separate places, it is called the out-of-body experience, or OBE.

In decades past, OBEs were the stuff of occult dogma, New Age doctrine, and tabloid journalism. More recently the experience has gained a kind of campy popularity, referenced on everything from ads for stereo headphones to sitcoms on TV. Published treatments of the subject often go to extremes. Those of mystical bent say it proves the existence of a soul that survives bodily death while many mainstream psychologists label it a hallucination, albeit one of vibrant, haunting beauty, brought on by relaxation, fatigue, or physiological stress.

In the midst of all this speculation many just don't realize that the OBE has been studied extensively in the lab. While the experience is not yet completely understood, science has gone a long way toward defining and demystifying this exquisite altered state of consciousness. It was in an effort to comprehend the experience that Keith Harary and his colleagues originally conducted the now-classic OBE experiments at Duke University in the early 1970s. Those groundbreaking experiments—the most detailed and extensive scientific exploration of the OBE to date—charted the psychophysiology of the experience and the state of alert relaxation at its root. They form the basis for this book.

As you work your way through the Free Flight Program, you will be tapping the insights gleaned from that seminal work, inducing the physiological and psychological state defined and studied in the Duke experiments. The OBE, Harary and colleagues found, could be achieved in their experiments through a paradoxical state of consciousness in which deep physical relaxation was accompanied by an underlying, heightened arousal. If the OBE is a physiological state, the research showed, it is also a compelling perceptual and communicative process—one that should be removed from the murky outback of occult claims and exposed to the bright light of mainstream science and everyday human experience.

Perhaps when we embrace this experience as a normal part of everyday life, we will come to a better understanding of what, precisely, it is. People who have had the experience say their focus of awareness literally seems to shift out of the body. They may feel as though they are hovering nearby, observing the body from above, or even rising through the rooftops, visiting distant friends and relatives, and traversing the globe. Most OBEers insist the experience is different from dreams or waking fantasies, and brain wave and other physiological measurements taken in the lab indicate this is so. According to some reports, OBE "travelers" can glimpse distant events and influence the behavior of distant people and animals.

Whatever it is, the out-of-body experience has been reported in one form or another through much of human history. In many cultures and religions, OBEs are viewed as a sign of advanced spiritual development, available only to those who embrace a mystical belief system, take certain drugs or maintain a special diet, pursue a vision quest, or chant mantras in a monastery from dawn to dusk. In some cultural and religious settings, OBEs are seen as harbingers of death—believed to carry those who have them into abstract levels of experience beyond physical reality where glimpses of the afterlife are perceived beyond the edges of the everyday real. Western science has often termed the experience a delusion, and nothing more.

We believe that OBEs may represent not one, but a variety of related altered states of consciousness, and that the key to unlocking their mystery will be found in conducting objective research into the nature of perception and the functioning of the brain. That said, we do not believe we must wait for the results of long-term research to explore the subjective dimensions of the OBE. Indeed, there is a certain wisdom in the ancient notion that OBEs can help you to increase your self-awareness and extend your boundaries of perception—even if you do not choose to embrace the specific beliefs of any particular culture or religion in relation to these experiences. You may not become a spiritual master by exploring OBEs, but you should gain a greater sense of mastery over your own inner life—including your ability to deal with ordinary stress. You may even find yourself discovering and exploring a fascinating realm of human experience in the process.

We believe that virtually anyone can have an OBE—provided they are receptive to the experience. The simple, thirty-day regimen outlined in the pages that follow will describe how you can begin to explore this experience for yourself. Based on research we and others have conducted at Duke University, at the Institute for Advanced Psychology, at the American Society for Psychical Research, and elsewhere, the Free Flight Program provides practical exercises designed to help you induce an OBE without subscribing to a mystical belief system, having a near death experience, or taking drugs. Of course, no one can absolutely guarantee that you'll have an OBE. But if you follow our guidelines, there's a good chance you'll be using OBEs to enhance your creativity and learning potential, reduce stress, and gain a new sense of inner freedom, no matter how constricting the circumstances of your everyday life. Used correctly, in fact, these straightforward exercises can help you embark upon truly breathtaking adventures free of charge and in the privacy of your own home!

You will start your journey in Week One by developing the psychological tools required for a successful OBE. First you will learn to pay more attention to your five senses, tuning into your relationship with your body and the subtleties of the surrounding world. You will also learn a crucial technique called alert relaxation, in which the body enters a state of deep relaxation while the mind remains acutely alert. This extraordinary state of mind has been effectively used by many people to explore a wide range of inner experiences—from mentally rehearsing an Olympic performance to stimulating the immune system. In our research experience, with the proper focus, it can be equally effective in inducing OBEs.

Week Two exercises, conducted in a state of alert relaxation, assist you in creating increasingly detailed mental images of distant sites.

As your ability to generate these images improves, you may feel yourself taking off, achieving the sensation of out-of-body flight.

Week Three exercises will teach you techniques for inducing OBEs with a partner or while falling asleep. The latter approach, in fact, may be one of the simplest means of inducing an alert relaxation state conducive to OBEs—once you have practiced the exercises presented in the earlier weeks of the Free Flight Program.

In Week Four of the Free Flight Program, you will focus on overcoming any remaining subconscious resistance to the OBE. Coordinating the skills you've developed during the first twenty-one days, you will learn practical techniques for inducing powerful OBEs at will.

In our experience, the best way to master the OBE is to begin a step at a time. Give yourself time to focus on each of the Free Flight exercises, and don't rush it. Although the program is designed to be carried out in thirty days, don't feel bound by this; it's perfectly acceptable to take longer to complete the program. So feel free to adapt our thirty-day approach to suit your own personal needs and schedule.

We do not recommend completing the program in less than thirty days, however, or trying to squeeze an entire week's worth of exercises into a single weekend. Although many of the Free Flight exercises are conceptually quite simple, their combined impact could be profound. Ultimately, you should have more control over your mental flights if your abilities evolve gradually, giving you an opportunity to adjust. Moreover, since the OBE tends to reflect your current mood, a balanced approach will reduce any turbulence and increase the pleasure of your Free Flight experiences.

The negative emotion Free Flight travelers most frequently report is fear—expressly, fear that if they "leave" the body they may not be able to "get back in." Such fear stems from the assumption that OBEs actually involve "leaving" the body in the first place. Though we still have much to learn about OBEs and the nature of human consciousness, scientific research has never proven that notion correct. Indeed, we do not believe that OBEs are external forces capable of overtaking and controlling you—and we do not believe that your mind literally leaves your body in the midst of the experience. Rather, we prefer to approach OBEs as states of awareness that you can induce and maintain of your own free will. You are never powerless during an OBE unless you believe you are, thereby creating a sense of powerlessness in yourself.

We advise you to think of the exercises that follow as a means of exploring an expansive, internal realm, thus empowering yourself with the knowledge and vision you previously lacked. If you're like many OBEers, you may eventually feel as though you have more control over the course of your OBEs than you do over many of the events in your everyday life.

Remember, if you should feel uncomfortable or fearful during any of these exercises, you can return to an ordinary waking state instantly just by remembering how it feels to be completely alert and aware of your body. If you have any doubts about your ability to comfortably handle OBEs, or to practice any of the exercises in the Free Flight Program, we encourage you to check with your doctor or therapist before proceeding.

To make the experience as enjoyable as possible, choose a practice location where you feel safe and won't be interrupted. We recommend sitting in an overstuffed or reclining chair, where you can relax without getting so cozy that you'll just fall asleep. Loosen any clothing or jewelry that makes you feel constricted. Take a deep breath before each practice session, allowing yourself a few moments to get grounded. Then be sure to quietly affirm that you'll only allow yourself to have experiences you can easily handle.

The more you relax and allow your mind to flow with the subtle shifts in perspective encouraged by the Free Flight exercises, the more likely you are to have an OBE. Do not try to force it. The most powerful OBEs often have a surprising quality. They can occur when you least expect them, at times when your attention is directed elsewhere. The Free Flight Program is designed to create a psychological setting in which these surprising experiences can occur. Any attempt to force the experience so that it takes on a prefabricated quality may interfere directly with this process and may possibly prevent you from discovering the unique elements of your own experiences that might otherwise spontaneously emerge. For this reason, we focus primarily on providing the essential tools that will help you explore the personal nature of your own OBEs for yourself, rather than suggesting that you construct and interpret the elements of your experiences in a particular fashion.

Please understand that OBEs may spontaneously emerge at any point in the Free Flight Program. Indeed, Free Flight is not a strictly linear process in which the goal is reached or not reached only at the end, and then it's over. Rather, this program is designed to interact, in an ongoing fashion, with each individual user. It helps set the appropriate internal conditions for an OBE, and can get things moving, but the exact timetable for OBE action is up to you. This means that OBEs may begin right away for one person; later on in the program for others; and after the program has been completed for others still.

No matter who you are, the Free Flight Program has been designed for your enjoyment. As you gain experience, you may start inducing OBEs in a variety of settings—a grassy hillside overlooking the Pacific or on the roof of a high rise in midtown Manhattan. You may induce different types of OBEs while listening to different types of music, or choose a different destination for your OBE with each passing day. In the end, you may allow your OBEs to emerge from the depths of your subconscious, revealing a host of hidden desires and possibilities. You may or may not have an OBE as you practice each of the individual exercises described below. But if you follow the entire Free Flight Program in a systematic way, you should greatly increase the quantity and quality of your OBEs.

Bon voyage!

WEEK ONE

GEARING UP

DAY 1 THROUGH THE LOOKING GLASS

DAY 2 ALTERED STATES

DAY 3 A SOUND APPROACH

DAY 4 "SCENTI-MENTAL JOURNEY"

DAY 5 THE LOUVRE METHOD

DAY 6 RETURN TICKET

DAY 7 LET'S GET PHYSICAL

WEEK ONE

GEARING UP

Having OBEs doesn't mean abandoning your body or giving up on your relationship with everyday reality. On the contrary, the experience should help you explore your relationship with your body and everyday reality on a more intense level than you may ever have thought possible. Indeed, the more relaxed and comfortable you feel toward your body and your surrounding environment, the easier it should be for you to induce out-of-body experiences at will.

We therefore start the Free Flight Program with an exercise aimed at intensifying your psychological relationship with your own body. As the week progresses, you will turn your attention outward, pursuing a deeper and more sensual relationship with your environment as well.

When you have completed Week One, you should have far greater conscious control over your body and the sensory input to which it responds. You should also become adept at mentally shifting your point of view from the inner realm to the outer realm and back.

Finally, during Week One you will immerse yourself in an altered state known as *alert relaxation*, in which the body is deeply relaxed while the mind remains acutely alert. Because alert relaxation induces a lowered level of awareness in the body and a heightened level of awareness in the mind, it can literally promote a feeling of separation between the two.

DAY 1

THROUGH THE LOOKING GLASS

The following exercise will help you celebrate your relationship with your body, gaining greater insight into the connection between your psychological and physical selves. Begin by standing completely naked in front of a full-length mirror with a light turned on behind you. Examine your body from head to toe and back again. As you study yourself, consider how completely familiar your body is to you, and how different you feel toward your own body than toward the bodies of those around you. Notice any scars or other unique or unusual identifying characteristics that you associate with your body. How do you recognize your body when you see yourself photographed among a large group of people? Is there a familiar smell that you associate with your body? How does the inside of your mouth taste right now? What has changed about your body, and what has remained consistent as you've grown older? What do you like about your body? What would you like to change?

As you continue standing in front of the mirror, close your eyes and slowly take a deep breath. Remember the way you appeared as you looked at yourself in the mirror. Take another deep breath and, as you exhale, open your eyes and look at your reflection. Inhale deeply once more, then close your eyes and again remember the way you looked when you saw yourself reflected in the mirror. Exhale slowly, open your eyes, and look back in the mirror. Notice the way your sense of yourself and of reality seems to subtly shift when you direct your attention outwardly toward your reflection, then inwardly toward your mental image of your body. This initial exercise should take you no longer than twenty or thirty minutes.

Flight Directive—Take a thirty-minute break before proceeding to the next exercise. Get dressed and go for a walk around the block or run some short errands that will help ground you in mundane reality. Pay particular attention to the way your body moves and feels as you go about your errands. Notice how easily, virtually unconsciously, you move a part of your body after deciding to do so. Feel your body responding to stream-of-consciousness thoughts as you perform such activities as walking, lifting, or driving a car.

When you return from your break, sit in a comfortable chair, preferably one that allows you to stretch out, and relax with your eyes opened. Take a deep breath and quietly notice the way your body feels relaxing in the chair. Pay attention to the feelings in your muscles, and the difference between how your body felt when you were active a short while earlier and how it feels now that you're beginning to relax. See if you can feel your heart beating in the center of your chest. Notice the way your heartbeat slows down as you become more and more relaxed. Pay attention to your breathing. Notice the way your breathing also slows down. Wiggle your fingers and toes. Contrast the sensations deep within your skeletal muscles to those on the surface of your skin.

Sit very still with your eyes open for ten or fifteen minutes and imagine that instead of experiencing reality as you normally do, via sensory organs on the surface of your body, you are perceiving the world from somewhere within your body. For instance, imagine that your eyes are transparent portholes through which your consciousness looks out at the world. Then feel yourself shrinking inside your body. Imagine yourself getting smaller and smaller, until your body feels like a rubber suit fitting loosely around your consciousness. Finally, when you feel comfortable doing so, breathe slowly and deeply and envision yourself gradually returning to normal size.

Flight Directive—Although you may feel eager to proceed directly into the next exercise, we recommend taking an overnight break. This is the best way to allow your subconscious mind to fully absorb the images already formed. Keep in mind, however, that as you progress through the Free Flight Program you may benefit by repeating this exercise, as well as others you've learned on previous days.

The exercise above, for instance, can be practiced at various times of the day just by relaxing and bringing to mind the images you had when you first learned it. You might try it the next time you find yourself waiting for a flight at the airport, sitting in a waiting room, or taking a ride on the subway. Repeating all the Free Flight exercises regularly is a good way of reinforcing their effects, so long as you otherwise go about your usual daily activities and proceed with the rest of the Free Flight Program in the prescribed way.

DAY 2

ALTERED STATES

You are now ready to learn the technique of alert relaxation, a skill that stress researchers and sports psychologists have long found useful in relieving tension and increasing concentration. This technique is also crucial to success in the Free Flight Program. As mentioned, alert relaxation enables your body to deeply relax while your mind stays acutely alert. When you become extremely relaxed, your body seems to recede into the background while the outside world draws most of your attention. By learning to remain highly alert in an intensely relaxed physical state, therefore, you can develop the ability to focus your awareness on distant locations without feeling overly restricted by your body or physical condition.

To begin, sit in a comfortable chair, stretch your muscles, and take a deep breath. Then imagine that warm currents of mental energy are very slowly moving up through your body. Proceed very slowly, allowing each muscle group to fully relax before sending the imaginary currents onto the next section of your body. Feel the muscles in your feet gradually warming and relaxing as you imagine the currents passing through them. Imagine that the currents very gradually continue moving up through your calves, into your thighs, through your hips and buttocks and into your lower back and abdomen.

Feel the muscles in your legs becoming heavy, warm, and relaxed as they sink down into the chair beneath you. When you feel your legs becoming deeply relaxed, imagine the currents moving in a clockwise motion around your abdomen, then up along your spine and through the front of your torso into your chest and shoulders. Feel the muscles in your stomach and lower back letting go of any tightness or tension as the current passes through them.

When the lower half of your body feels deeply relaxed, imagine the currents flowing upward through your ribs and shoulders, warming and relaxing the upper part of your body, leaving your back and chest completely warm and free of any stress or tension. Imagine the currents turning around to move downward through your arms, toward your fingertips, swirling around through your fingers and hands, then moving upward once more and back through your arms and neck toward the top of your head.

Now feel the muscles in your neck and face gradually growing warm and relaxed as the imaginary currents pass through them. Then imagine the currents flowing out through the top of your head, leaving your entire body feeling comfortably warm, heavy, and relaxed.

Allow your body to sink down into the chair beneath you. As you do, you may notice some inner part of you becoming lighter as your body feels heavier and heavier. You may even begin to feel a slight sensation of floating above your body. If you find yourself having such feelings, don't analyze or attempt to directly influence them. Just allow them to evolve on their own.

Remember, the key to success here is learning to enter a state of deep physical relaxation while remaining mentally alert. But if you should find yourself accidentally falling asleep while practicing this exercise, don't worry about it. The moment you wake up and realize what has happened, just continue the exercise, without moving, from wherever you left off. At this point you'll probably already be quite relaxed, so the key will be to become even more deeply relaxed without once more falling asleep.

In order to remain alert, you may find it helpful to imagine the warm currents passing through your body in a variety of colors and patterns. You may also find it helpful to practice this exercise only when you are physically and emotionally rested and easily able to remain awake for the entire exercise.

Once you have achieved a deeply relaxed, mentally alert

state, you should attempt to sustain it for anywhere from fifteen to thirty minutes. For most people, the state of alert relaxation will end spontaneously within that time frame. However, if you remain in this altered state for more than thirty minutes on Day 2, we suggest that you intentionally bring yourself out of it. (Of course, if you should find yourself spontaneously having an out-of-body experience at any point while practicing the alert relaxation exercise, just enjoy the experience without worrying about the time.)

There are two basic ways to interrupt the state of alert relaxation: one is to become less alert; the other is to become less relaxed.

Becoming less alert simply means finally allowing yourself to drift off into sleep. This approach has its advantages: during our more than nineteen years of research in this field, we have found that people often have spontaneous out-of-body experiences from a sleep state after practicing the alert relaxation exercise on a regular basis.

To interrupt the state of alert relaxation without falling asleep, we suggest that you wiggle your fingers and toes, slowly stretch your muscles, then sit up and look around the room. Touch the arms of the chair to make solid contact with waking reality before getting up and walking around. Move your arms and legs and feel the solidity of your body. While you may find this an elaborate method for simply getting up after relaxing in a chair, it is, in fact, a good way to train yourself for later making a comfortable and gradual reentry into ordinary waking reality following an OBE.

We suggest that you practice this exercise at least once a day for the remainder of the thirty days of the Free Flight Program. What's more, to master the technique of alert relaxation as quickly and completely as possible, we recommend that, initially, at least, you ask a friend to help by slowly and quietly reading the above relaxation instructions aloud. You may also wish to tape these instructions so that you can practice on your own after the initial session.

Once you gain experience, you'll probably be able to enter this state more and more quickly without the need for any formal instructions at all. As you continue to perfect your alert relaxation technique, you may find that remaining alert while entering a deeply relaxed physical state can create the sensation that your mind is somehow separated from your body. This sensation can be the most subtle or preliminary form of the out-of-body experience.

Flight Directive—During the next few days, you'll be working on a technique called *sensory focusing.* This method, developed by pioneers in the human-potential movement back in the Sixties, will help you become aware of all your senses; you will eventually learn to concentrate on any individual sense or combination of senses at any given time. You will also learn to focus your senses on particular aspects of your environment. When practiced in conjunction with alert relaxation, sensory focusing can help you induce out-of-body experiences from a waking state. It can also be used to exert control over your OBEs once they occur.

DAY 3

A SOUND APPROACH

Day 3 focuses on your sense of hearing. We're intentionally beginning with a nonvisual sense because most of us direct so much of our perceptual attention toward visual information that we often allow it to overwhelm the input of our other senses. By first practicing with a nonvisual sense such as hearing, you won't be as likely to let visual information overwhelm you and reduce the input of other perceptions while you are in the midst of an OBE.

Begin this exercise sitting quietly in an active and stimulating location, such as a bench in a downtown plaza, the lobby of a museum, or the waiting area of a train station. Take a deep breath and try to discern the inner sound of your heartbeat. Then listen to the sound of your breathing. Finally, as you continue to sense your heartbeat and breathing, expand your focus of attention to include the other sounds in your immediate environment. Keep your eyes open throughout this exercise, but don't look at the sources of the sounds you're hearing unless this is absolutely unavoidable.

When you feel comfortable, start to move around your environment on foot. As you move about, continue to pay close attention to your heartbeat and breathing as well as the sounds encountered in your environment. Concentrating on these sounds, try to ignore any nonauditory sensations, except, of course, those essential for safe navigation. Again, avoid looking in the direction of any sounds you hear unless it is absolutely necessary.

Pay attention to the layers of sound that surround you. Notice how certain sounds draw your immediate attention while others fade into the background. Concentrate on those sounds that are closest to you, then on those farther away. Then concentrate on the loudest or most dramatic sounds, followed by the smaller and more subtle sounds you don't usually notice. Repeat these steps until you're able to focus on any particular sound while deliberately excluding other sounds from your immediate awareness. Finally, listen to various combinations of sounds, and to all the sounds around you at once, without losing track of any individual sound.

Flight Directive—Spend a minimum of one or two hours practicing this auditory focusing exercise. When you're through, take a break for a few hours. Then review and practice the alert relaxation technique you learned on Day 2.

DAY 4

"SCENTIMENTAL JOURNEY"

Day 4 will help you fine-tune your senses of smell and taste. Since you'll begin by focusing on your sense of smell, we ask that you not eat lunch or dinner before practicing this part of the exercise. (Food you've eaten can sometimes influence your perception of smells in the environment; what's more, perceptions during the taste part of the exercise will be more intense if you've abstained from eating for a while.)

As you did for the hearing exercise on Day 3, start by sitting quietly in an active and interesting location. The place you choose should not be the same spot you selected for the hearing exercise, but should be a *new* environment, one rich with many interesting smells. Good choices would be an open-air market, an amusement park by the beach, a department store, or the elephant house at your local zoo. Find a spot where you can sit quietly, take a deep breath, and relax. Concentrate on the information that's coming to you through your sense of smell alone.

Concentrate first on the familiar smell of your own body. Do you regularly wear perfume or cologne, or anything else that gives you a recognizable scent? You may find that your sense of smell has become dulled to this familiar aroma. Shortly after you splash on cologne, for example, you may no longer notice it, even though the others around you detect the scent quite easily. Rub your palms on the part of you where the scent should be the strongest, then hold your hands up to your nose and breathe deeply. Notice how the scent becomes stronger for a moment, then once again seems to fade.

Are there other familiar smells that you associate with your body? Smell your clothes, for example, and notice the scent of your detergent. If you're wearing a jacket or coat, does it smell different from the shirt or sweater you're wearing under it? Unbutton your top button or pull out your collar, and put your nose inside of it so that you can smell your skin. Does the inside of your shirt smell different from the outside?

Now focus on your immediate environment. Allow the familiar smells of your body to fade into the background as other nearby smells come into prominence. Without closing your eyes, turning your head, or moving from your initial spot, what are the strongest smells you notice in your nearby surroundings?

When you feel ready, begin moving around the special

location you've chosen for this exercise. As you move about, focus on the variety of smells around you. Use your other senses to direct you toward as many interesting smells as possible, but don't just concentrate on the smells that are closest to you. Instead, try to focus on a variety of smells at varying distances from your body. Use your own familiar smell as a reference point to focus your attention in more closely, then use distant smells to focus your attention farther and farther away. Notice how some smells seem to draw your immediate interest, while others are more subtle and seem to be easily overpowered or to fade into the background of your environment.

> ***Flight Directive***—Spend a minimum of thirty minutes to an hour focusing on your sense of smell in this fashion. Then break for about fifteen or twenty minutes before moving on. To ensure a gap of no more than twenty minutes between the first and second parts of this exercise, we suggest that you conduct both parts in approximately the same locale.

Now it's time to focus on your sense of taste. For your dining pleasure, we have designed this exercise to take place during a meal. We suggest eating in a restaurant for this exercise, rather than at home, because we want you to focus on your sense of taste rather than on cooking and doing the dishes. We also don't want you to be exposed to the food you'll be eating before carrying out the exercise. (If you prefer, however, you can also conduct this exercise at home by asking someone else to prepare the food.)

If you do decide to eat out, we recommend that you select a place offering a wide variety of surprising taste sensations, such as an ethnic delicatessen or a Chinese or Indian restaurant. As an alternative, you might go to a tourist attraction, such as San Francisco's Fisherman's Wharf or New York's Coney Island; such places generally offer a wide assortment of fast-food stands representing many different cuisines. In any case, order a meal designed to give you as varied a combination of taste experiences as possible, even if you have to take most of it home after tasting it to avoid indigestion.

We suggest your meal include foods you haven't tasted

before. It should also include foods that wouldn't ordinarily go together in a single meal. One combination, for instance, might be hot peppers, lime Jell-O, gefilte fish, eggrolls, pizza, pastrami on rye, cranberry juice, split pea soup, chocolate eclairs, and kippers. Of course, you shouldn't eat anything that violates the requirements of any restricted diet prescribed by your doctor. Make sure that you also have plenty of water, bread, or crackers available to clear your palate between courses.

When the food arrives, relax, look it over and imagine what the various dishes will taste like. Take a deep breath and taste the inside of your mouth before you start eating. Then taste something sweet, rinse out your mouth with some water, and taste something salty. Rinse out your mouth again and taste something hot and spicy, followed by something mild and cool.

Continue in this way, gradually tasting things and clearing your palate, so that your taste buds have time to readjust before you stimulate them again. To avoid getting sick from eating too many strange combinations, we recommend that you only take small bites and don't swallow everything. Notice how the inside of your mouth tastes at various points in this exercise, and how certain tastes become overwhelmed by others. Notice, also, how your sense of taste is closely related to your sense of smell. You can almost taste some foods without eating them because they have such strong aromas.

Although tasting a bizarre combination of foods may seem at first like a strange way of inducing OBEs, this exercise is actually helping you focus on one of your most important senses. Your sense of taste may not guide you through life as directly as vision or hearing, but it does influence much of your relationship with your body. Consider how much time you spend eating or thinking about food on a daily basis, and how strongly you may focus on your sense of taste right before, during, and after a meal. Consider, also, how your other senses may become temporarily overwhelmed by your sense of taste, particularly when you're really hungry.

Flight Directive—Spend at least an hour focusing on your sense of taste. Then take a break and practice alert relaxation for at least thirty minutes.

DAY 5

THE LOUVRE METHOD

The Louvre Method was named after the experience of writer Darlene Moore, who first practiced this exercise one afternoon in the courtyard of the Louvre Museum in Paris. That night, as she lay on her bed in her hotel room on the Left Bank, she sensed herself separating from her body. Moments later, she felt as if she were literally looking back at her body lying on the bed from across the room. She had just had her first spontaneous out-of-body experience.

The exercise put Moore in touch with her sensory experiences; it enabled her to intensively explore not just hearing, smell, and taste, but vision and the sense of touch as well. By becoming more aware of the sensations associated with her body, she was, paradoxically, able to open her unconscious mind to the possibility of having an OBE.

To practice the Louvre Method, you'll need a companion to help guide you through the exercise. Begin by choosing a location rich in a variety of forms, textures, and sounds. This should not be a location that you've used for any other part of the Free Flight Program, or even a place where you've spent time on other occasions. A plaza, park, or beach would all be very good choices for this exercise.

Your eyes should remain closed for the entire session, which should take at least two hours to complete. (We suggest that you wear a pair of sunglasses so that you attract less attention from strangers around you.) You and your companion are not to talk to each other or anyone else for the duration of the exercise. Instead, your companion should use gentle, direct physical contact to guide you safely around the area and offer you a selection of stimulating nonvisual sensory experiences.

Stand with your companion at one end of the site you've selected. Then take a deep breath and close your eyes. Pay deliberate attention to the sound of your own breathing as well as to the sounds around you. As you did with the hearing exercise, try to perceive the sounds in multiple layers that overlap and blend with one another. (Notice the difference between the way you sense sound with your eyes closed and the way you sensed sound during the Day 3 exercise, when your eyes were open.) Take a few moments to absorb these layers of sound, then signal your companion that you're ready to proceed by tapping his or her shoulder.

Your companion should provide you with a variety of contrasting and surprising sensory experiences, taking special care to guide you safely around your environment. He or she may, for example, introduce you to a running fountain by placing your hand under it. Listen to the sound of the fountain, slowly run your hands along the edge, then feel the surface of the water. Your companion may then surprise you with a contrasting experience by, for example, offering you a handful of fragrant dried leaves to smell and slowly crumble in your hands. Listen to the leaves as you crumble them, feel their texture, and continue to notice the sounds of your breathing. Notice how the leaves feel and smell subtly different before and after you crumble them in your hands.

Throughout the exercise your companion should stimulate all your nonvisual senses, paying particular attention to the tactile realm. You, on the other hand, must explore your physical senses as though you had never done so before.

Be curious. As your companion guides you around, use your sense of hearing, smell, touch, and taste to communicate with selected aspects of your environment in a special way. Notice how your sense of yourself and reality slightly shifts each time you focus your attention on a different sense, or combination of senses.

After an hour to an hour and a half, your companion should instruct you to open your eyes. Sit in a shady spot, so that your eyes won't be bothered by the light. If you have been wearing sunglasses, take them off now. Take a deep breath, open your eyes, and notice the ways in which your awareness of yourself and your environment subtly shifts in that moment. Take a few minutes to adjust to your overall experience and to visually observe the immediate area surrounding you.

Concentrate on the full range of visual information that floods your senses the moment you open your eyes. Notice how your sudden focus on your sense of vision changes the way you relate to and interpret the input of all your other senses. Have your companion take you around to the spots where you practiced the nonvisual part of this exercise and show you the things you experienced earlier. Now concentrate on gathering as much visual information as possible, noticing the tiniest details and the way these details combine to form a greater visual whole. For instance, notice the veins in the crumbled leaves and the ripples in the fountain. As in the earlier part of this exercise, you and your companion should not talk to each other, but should instead communicate nonverbally as you explore the visual realm.

Now sit in the center of the area you've chosen and take a deep breath. Notice the way you perceive color. What colors have you chosen to wear for this occasion? What colors can be seen in your immediate environment? As you cast your eyes farther afield, what colors do you see?

As you look into the distance, notice the way the world around you seems to narrow and fade into the horizon. A grain of sand in your immediate area can become more or less personally significant than a mountain in the distance, depending entirely upon where you focus your visual attention.

Take a deep breath, and flood your senses with all that surrounds you. Don't analyze any of these perceptions, but allow them to completely flow through you. Then pay attention to various combinations of senses. Focus, for example, on your senses of smell and hearing. If you are at the beach, listen to the waves crashing on the sand and smell the wetness all around you. Now focus on vision and taste. Glimpse the shifting patterns of light in the waves and taste the salt in the air. Now focus on touch and hearing. Listen to nearby sounds and sounds in the distance; at the same time, feel your clothes against your skin and the sand beneath you.

Flight Directive—After completing the Louvre Method, take a break and spend the rest of the day having fun or carrying out activities that don't involve the Free Flight Program. This will give your mind a chance to integrate the experiences you've had today without wearing you out.

DAY 6

RETURN TICKET

Day 6 begins with the alert relaxation exercise you've been practicing throughout the week. Find a comfortable and psychologically secure location where you won't be disturbed and sit down and relax. Close your eyes, breathe deeply, and very slowly go through the stages of alert relaxation. As you become more and more relaxed, keep your attention focused solidly on the immediate environment.

As soon as you're feeling fully relaxed, remember the sensations you had yesterday, when you first practiced the Louvre Method. Imagine that you're back at that same place now, mentally exploring and experiencing your environment, this time without bringing your body along.

Listen to the sound of your breathing and imagine that you're listening to this sound in the same spot where you began the exercise on Day 5. Imagine that you can feel the ground beneath you, and the air on your face. Allow your memories of these sounds and feelings to fully form in your mind. Imagine that you are really back in that distant place *now* rather than just remembering the way it was *then*. Then, when these sensations have become fully formed in your mind, imagine that you're moving around and exploring that distant location.

Mentally "visit" the same spots that you visited yesterday when your companion guided you around the area. Remember the sounds you heard, the things you touched and smelled, and how close you felt to even the tiniest details of your environment. Remember the experience that surprised you there, and imagine that you're being surprised once again. Imagine that you are experiencing this distant location without a body, but that you are still able to have the same kinds of sensory experiences you had when you were physically present at the location. Notice how even your imaginary journey can shift its dimensions when you focus on different types of sensory experiences and different aspects of the distant environment.

Don't try to "open your eyes" while on this imaginary journey. Instead, recall the visual experience you had when you were physically present at the location, allowing your mental experience to emerge directly from there. In addition, as you continue your imaginary journey, try to "move about" the distant environment by focusing on different spots. Notice that to get from one spot to the next, you need not actually traverse the distance between the two. You can, instead, just "pop" out of one locale and into the next. This is an example of the many ways in which OBEs don't always obey the laws of everyday reality.

Spend at least an hour practicing this exercise. Then, when you feel ready to conclude your imaginary journey, just remember all the images and sensations that you associate with your body. Remember the way your body appeared when you looked at yourself in the mirror on Day 1, and how it smelled when you carried out the sensory focusing exercises later in the week. Remember how aware you are of your body and immediate surroundings whenever you practice alert relaxation. Take a deep breath and slowly wiggle your fingers and toes, stretch your muscles, then sit up and look around the room. Touch your own arms and the arms of the chair; feel the solidness of mundane reality, and get up and walk around.

You may find, as you conduct this imaginary journey, that you have achieved the sensation of floating apart from your body. Instead of trying to figure out whether you're really having an OBE, you may find it more helpful to just allow the experience to emerge.

Flight Directive—As you progress through the Free Flight Program, we strongly suggest that you keep a balanced perspective by otherwise going about your usual routines in a normal way. Do not withdraw from reality. We also recommend that you practice alert relaxation combined with the Return Ticket technique on a daily basis.

DAY 7

LET'S GET PHYSICAL

You should begin Day 7 by inducing a state of alert relaxation. While in that state, spend about an hour practicing the Return Ticket exercise you learned on Day 6. Remember, focus your attention on the location at which you first practiced the Louvre Method.

After completing your imaginary journey, spend at least one hour pursuing some kind of rigorous physical activity. This will balance the amount of attention you've been paying to your mental experience, providing healthy, nonanalytic physical conditioning. Depending upon your physical situation and personal preferences you may decide to jog, walk, work out at the gym, wash the car, or play a game of basketball with the neighborhood crowd.

When you feel satisfied with the amount of physical exercise you've gotten, spend some time enjoying the best that mundane reality has to offer. Get close to a friend or loved one, enjoy a good meal, do some chores around the house, go for a drive in the country, or see a movie. Pretend that today is a personal holiday and do something to make it special. Remember, you have something to celebrate. You've completed the first week of the Free Flight Program!

WEEK ONE ROUNDUP GEARING UP

DAY 1 THROUGH THE LOOKING GLASS	**DAY 2** ALTERED STATES	**DAY 3** A SOUND APPROACH	**DAY 4** "SCENTI-MENTAL JOURNEY"	
Study your body in the mirror. Feel a range of inner sensations. Imagine your consciousness shrinking and expanding within you. Shift your focus of attention in and out of your body.	Sit in your chair. Imagine energy currents flowing through your body. Deeply relax your muscles. Sustain an acutely alert conscious state. Enter the altered state of alert relaxation. Return to the everyday state of alert waking consciousness.	Sit quietly in an active location. Listen to internal sounds like your heartbeat and your breathing. Focus upon sounds in the environment around you. Move around on foot, focusing on sounds and ignoring most other sensations. Learn to focus on particular sounds to the exclusion of others.	Sit quietly in a location rich in many smells. Smell your own body. Focus on odors in the environment. Move around, guided by a medley of odors. Go to a restaurant or any other outdoor or indoor eatery. Order a meal designed to offer a wide variety of taste sensations. Taste it all.	

	DAY 5 THE LOUVRE METHOD	**DAY 6** RETURN TICKET	**DAY 7** LET'S GET PHYSICAL
	Go to a new and richly textured environment with a friend. With the help of your friend, explore this environment for at least an hour with your eyes closed. Open your eyes. Now explore this environment with your eyes open.	Induce the altered state of alert relaxation. Imagine the richly textured site you visited on Day 5. Mentally visit the area, reexperiencing the sensations of the day. Try to move about this environment in your mind by focusing on a variety of specific locations. After an hour, return to alert waking consciousness.	Enter a state of alert relaxation. Imagine the locale you visited on Day 5. Spend at least one hour involved in intense physical activity. Have some fun.

WEEK TWO

TAKING OFF

WEEK TWO

•

TAKING OFF

Welcome to Week Two of the Free Flight Program! Week Two exercises should help catapult you into the expanded realm of the OBE. First, Week Two exercises will help you shift your psychological perspective as you relate to your body and the surrounding world. This ability is particularly important because it will help you simulate the most important aspect of an actual out-of-body experience: the subjective sensation of existing apart from your body.

As the week goes on, you will learn how to shift your attention to distant locations, and even back and forth in time. As you hone these psychological skills, you can develop the OBEer's uncanny sense of mental navigation.

You will also begin to learn which techniques make the OBE most feasible for *you*. Some participants may take to Free Flight after envisioning their consciousness at a point across the room, while others will most easily have OBEs by imagining a past or future time. Finally, no matter what your natural bent, during Week Two we will teach you how to overcome your limitations, so that you may learn to experience virtually any type of OBE at all.

Week Two exercises will help you overcome your limitations by defeating the one major impediment to OBEs: fear of leaving the body, never to return. Indeed, by the time you have completed Week Two of the Free Flight Program, you will know that the OBE does not necessarily involve the perception of a second body that somehow separates or "peels off" from the first. You will know that OBEs do not require that you fly around from one locale to the next, like a restless ghost evacuating a dead body. And you will know that OBEs are not stereotypical experiences stamped from a cookie-cutter mold. Rather, they are as mundane or surprising in their content as you allow them to be for you.

DAY 8

RISING ABOVE IT

On Day 8 you will begin to develop a basic skill: the ability to imagine your mind and body existing in two separate places. This exercise can psychologically prepare you for an OBE; ultimately it can also help you induce the experience at will.

Begin by lying in a comfortable, quiet, and secure location. Then induce a state of alert relaxation. Once you have achieved a deeply relaxed yet alert physical and mental state, notice how it feels to be "inside" your body. Notice, as you did during Week One, how it feels to "look" through your closed eyelids and how you can focus your attention on the world around you from "inside" your physical form. Once again, imagine yourself gradually becoming smaller within your body. Then imagine your consciousness expanding out to fill the entire room. Finally, imagine yourself returning to your normal size and take a deep breath. Quietly pay attention to the sounds and sensations that you associate with breathing.

Now stay perfectly still and, as you exhale, imagine how it would feel to be a few inches above your physical form. Imagine that you are simultaneously floating above your body and also looking up at your floating image from within your body. Allow yourself time to fully create these images in your mind. Then gradually begin moving your attention back and forth between the inside of your body and the point you envision a few inches above.

Continue practicing until you're able to imagine floating above yourself for several minutes without straining. Once you've accomplished this, imagine your disembodied face looking back at your physical face, below. Practice focusing as little attention as possible on your body and as much as possible on the image of yourself floating above. Create as complete an image as possible until—perhaps for only an instant—detailed visual, tactile, and auditory impressions from this slightly altered perspective become vivid enough to seem real.

The sensation of looking back at your physical body from an independent location directly above it is one of the most basic and commonly reported forms of the out-of-body experience. Once you have achieved this perception, we suggest that you gradually shift your awareness back to the familiar sensations that you associate with your body.

Flight Directive—After practicing this exercise, take a break for an hour. Then repeat the entire session from the beginning. But this time, maintain the image of floating for ten or fifteen minutes. Later, as you're lying in bed at the end of the day, imagine floating above your body as you fall asleep. For the rest of the Free Flight Program, this last step should be a nightly routine.

DAY 9

A ROOM WITH A VIEW

For this exercise, use the same comfortable, secure location you used the day before. Lie down and induce a state of alert relaxation. As soon as you feel deeply relaxed, concentrate on the sounds and internal sensations that you associate with breathing, and once more try to perceive the world from "within" your body.

This time, instead of imagining that you're floating directly above your body, focus your attention on a specific location across the room. Imagine your awareness moving away from your body toward that slightly distant part of your environment.

Now imagine that you're a point of consciousness floating on the other side of the room, and that you're looking back at your body from this new and more remote perspective. Take time to allow this perception to form in your imagination. Focus on this imagined experience in your mind's eye, trying to capture the details with input from all five senses.

After a few minutes, shift your focus to a completely different part of your immediate environment. Allow the details of this new location to fully form in your imagination as the impressions associated with the earlier location slowly dissolve. Maintain this new focus for several minutes before gradually shifting your attention back to your body.

As you perform this exercise, take the time to create images that are as vivid as possible. The more detailed your images, the more likely you will be to have an OBE.

> ***Flight Directive***—After practicing this exercise, break for thirty minutes or more. Then, if you feel like it, repeat this exercise and continue to focus your perceptions at increasingly greater distances from your body. You may repeat this procedure up to three successive times. Remember, no matter how many times you repeat this exercise, do not rush through it.

DAY 10

BEING THERE

During spontaneous out-of-body experiences, many people report feeling as though they are visiting places that have a strong emotional attraction for them. These may be familiar places, or they may be less familiar sites with symbolic or personal significance. By recognizing and envisioning the locations most significant to you, you may be able to induce an OBE.

Flight Directive—Today you will perform the most complex of the Free Flight exercises. We suggest that you read the instructions over two or three times before you begin. If, while performing the exercise, you leave out a step or two, don't worry about it. The cumulative effect of carrying out most of the steps will be a powerful tool for inducing an OBE.

On Day 10, begin by choosing an indoor location with particular meaning to you. Once you have chosen your spot, find a comfortable outdoor location about ten or fifteen minutes' walking distance from that spot. Go to that outdoor location and stand with your eyes closed. As you stand there take a deep breath, then imagine that you are home lying in the comfortable chair in which you practiced the relaxation exercises of Week One. Slowly open your eyes and imagine that everything you're physically experiencing is part of an intense out-of-body experience. Take another deep breath, look around at your immediate surroundings, and absorb the full impact of your environment.

Continue to experience your surroundings as you proceed, at a leisurely pace, toward the indoor location you've chosen. Remember, you're still pretending to be in the midst of an OBE. Thus, you should avoid all human contact unless it's absolutely necessary. It might even help to think of yourself as a ghost.

When you arrive at the indoor spot, continue to imagine that you are in the midst of an OBE. This means you must assume the role of the observer. If you are visiting your office in the middle of the night, for example, you are not there to go through papers or take the opportunity to catch up on your work. If you are visiting your bedroom in the middle of the day, this is not the time to straighten up the place or make the bed you left buried under a mountain of tangled sheets and blankets in the morning.

Instead, maintain a sense of objective distance from your surroundings, as though you were visiting a museum exhibit of a significant place in your life. Imagine that you are visiting this place for the very first time. What do the tiniest details tell you about the emotional atmosphere of the place? What kinds of people live or work there? How would they react to your "ghostlike" presence right now?

Now take a deep breath and examine this location in a more personal way. What's the difference between this place during its "off hours" and during the time you're most accustomed to being there? Imagine how it might be to have an out-of-body experience in which you felt as though you were "visiting" this location at its most active time of day. Then focus once again on the difference between your usual experience in this environment and the way you're experiencing it now during your imaginary OBE.

After you've spent fifteen or twenty minutes in this indoor location, return to the outdoor site where you first began the exercise. Once again, avoid any interactions with people as you continue to focus on your surroundings. Take a deep breath, close your eyes for a moment, and imagine that you're home in your comfortable chair. Then open your eyes and return home as quickly as possible.

The moment you get home, and before speaking to anyone or involving yourself in any other activities, immediately kick off your shoes and sit back in the chair where you practiced the alert relaxation exercise during Week One. Gradually enter a state of alert relaxation, focusing on the outdoor location from which you've just returned. Recall in vivid detail the way you felt while you were standing there with your eyes closed and imagining that you were at home in the chair.

Now take a deep breath and imagine that you are back at the indoor location. Remember the way you felt while you were absorbing the details of this familiar place. Allow yourself to fully absorb this memory, then take another deep breath and imagine that you are back at the outdoor location. Remember how you felt while you were standing outdoors, absorbing the sensory impact of your surroundings and imagining that your body was back at home in the chair.

Now it is time to emerge from your state of alert relaxation. Take a deep breath, slowly wiggle your fingers and toes, and open your eyes. Feel the solidity of your body and the arms of the chair before getting up and moving about the room.

> ***Flight Directive***—Take a break of at least several hours after practicing this exercise. To help ground you in everyday reality, do something mundane and ordinary, like watching your favorite television show, taking the dog for a long walk, having a pizza delivered, or going out to a movie.

Now practice this exercise again, using the same outdoor location as your intermediary focus, but a different indoor location for your imaginary OBE "visit." If you used your bedroom as your focus during the middle of the day, for example, you might consider using your office as the emotional focus of a second session to be carried out in the early or late evening.

> ***Flight Directive***—If practicing this exercise seems at all disorienting, keep in mind that this is in keeping with its overall purpose. Ideally, as you proceed through the Free Flight Program and continue practicing the various exercises on a regular basis, you'll develop the ability to focus on any location without being excessively limited by your immediate physical surroundings.

DAY 11

SHOPPING SPREE

Today you will take a break from the spatial focusing exercises of the past three days. Instead, Day 11 will teach you to focus not on places, but on individual objects, both familiar and strange.

Begin by going to a department store or shopping center you've never visited before. For the first part of this exercise, your goal will be to pick a small section of the shopping area and explore the various displays of objects for sale without buying anything. As in earlier exercises, this should be a private experience; thus, you must keep your direct interactions with other people to a minimum. As you examine and handle various objects, notice how impersonal your response to these objects can be when you have no intention of buying them. A coffeepot is just another coffeepot if you have no intention of taking it home to your kitchen; a screwdriver is just another screwdriver if you have no intention of buying and using it. Spend thirty or forty-five minutes handling various objects in the section of the shopping area you have chosen.

> ***Flight Directive***—Now take a twenty-minute break by going out for refreshments before returning to the store or shopping center.

When you return to the shopping area, pick a different section to browse through. Your goal this time will be to shop for a small gift, an object that costs no more than ten or fifteen dollars, for a special person in your life.

Notice how your emotional response to the objects around you is altered as you experience them in relation to your feelings about a particular person. Notice, also, how your response to the object you finally select is altered by your perception of it as a gift for the person you have in mind.

After you've purchased the object and left the store, take it out of its wrappings and look at it. The object may be one of thousands just like it in form and function, yet it has now become uniquely meaningful in and of itself because of the emotional significance you attach to it. Take the object home with you and place it in a prominent location where you can look at it for a while before giving it to the person you have in mind. Sit across the room from the object, relax, and remember the moment when you first noticed the object in the store. Focus strictly, for a moment, on the object's basic form and function. Then shift your focus toward the emotional significance of the object as a gift for someone you care about. Continue slowly shifting your emotional focus toward the object back and forth in this fashion for at least fifteen minutes.

> ***Flight Directive***—Take a short break before proceeding to the next part of this exercise.

After your break, take an exploratory journey around your home. Begin by focusing on your home as you remember it was just before you moved in. Remember how empty and foreign it seemed, and how different it began to feel as you filled it with your familiar objects. Now observe the objects all around you in your home. Select individual objects that have some special meaning for you, and remember the first time you encountered them. Then remember what made the objects special to you and how familiar a part of your environment they've become over time. Consider the total impact of your feelings toward *all* the objects around you. How do these objects influence your reaction to your home environment?

For the next phase of this exercise, enter a state of alert relaxation. Close your eyes and focus on the gift you brought home from the store. Imagine that you are floating in the air in front of the gift, wherever it may be. Concentrate on the smallest details of your gift, on its form and function as an object, and on its emotional significance in your life. Imagine that you are no larger than a tiny dot, and that you can see the object from a very close-up perspective looming all around you. Then imagine that you are your usual size, observing the object from a distance.

Take a deep breath and think about another significant personal object in your home environment (other than the gift). Focus on your feelings toward this personal object, and on the tiniest details of its form, even details you don't usually notice. Imagine yourself floating in the air in front of the familiar object. Imagine yourself as a tiny dot in space with the object becoming larger than life, then imagine yourself returning to normal size. Take a deep breath, let it out slowly, and notice the feelings of your body.

For the next thirty minutes, focus on a variety of emotionally significant objects in your home using the instructions above.

Flight Directive—Take a break for the rest of the day, involving youself in activities unrelated to the Free Flight Program. Also, before falling asleep, please read the instructions for the first part of tomorrow's exercise, which must be practiced first thing in the morning.

Later on in the evening, as you're going to sleep, imagine looking back at your body, lying below. Then remember any emotionally significant objects around your home, including the gift you bought earlier, and allow yourself to drift off to sleep.

DAY 12

WITHIN YOU AND WITHOUT YOU

You must do the following exercise the first thing in the morning, before you get out of bed. As soon as you notice yourself emerging from sleep, before you even open your eyes or move, concentrate on the image of your face looking back at you. Take your time and allow the image of your face to fully form in your imagination. Then take a deep breath and imagine one of the emotionally signficant objects you focused on yesterday. Once again, imagine that you're floating in the air in front of the object you've selected.

Concentrate on your memories of the object and its immediate surroundings; recall the aesthetic details of the object and the way in which its function may be expressed in even the tiniest aspects of its form. Continue to see yourself floating near the object as you consider its place in your life.

Take another deep breath and envision the area adjacent to your body. Allow the significant object to fade from your immediate awareness and concentrate once again on the image of your face looking back at you. As you did on Day 8, imagine that you're floating in the air above your bed, looking down at your body lying below.

Now take another deep breath. Wiggle your fingers and toes, and open your eyes. As soon as you feel comfortable, you may begin your usual morning activities.

Flight Directive—For the rest of the day, just go about your usual activities. You may practice some of the Free Flight exercises, if an appropriate opportunity presents itself.

Later in the evening, when you're back in bed and falling asleep, focus on the image of your own face looking back at you. Also concentrate on the images of significant objects around your home. Then, as you're waking up the next day, repeat the exercise as you practiced it this morning.

> ***Flight Directive***—Now that you've learned Day 12 exercises, you should incorporate them into your morning and evening routines on a regular basis. As you proceed, you may use virtually any object you wish.

DAY 13

UNFINISHED BUSINESS

Day 13 of the Free Flight Program gives you another opportunity to use familiar objects to help induce an out-of-body experience. But while you focused on emotionally significant objects in the previous exercise, you will now direct your attention toward the seemingly insignificant objects that nonetheless form the backdrop of your environment.

Begin simply by noticing the objects that you take for granted in your home and workplace. It isn't necessary to examine any of these objects closely unless you want to; but it is important to directly acknowledge their presence, even if only for a moment.

It is almost inevitable that, sometime during the first phase of this exercise, you will notice some familiar object that somehow seems slightly out of place. The object may, for example, be a crooked picture on your office wall, a book positioned oddly on a shelf, or a tube of toothpaste that you forgot to put away the day before. When you first focus on the object, your impulse will probably be to return it to its proper position or place.

Resist the impulse.

Instead, leave the object alone, pausing for a few moments

to notice how your restraint makes you feel on a deep, inner level. Imagine the way the object "should" be placed, and how it would look in its proper position. Focus on what it is specifically about the object's present position that makes it seem out of place.

As the day proceeds, notice the misplaced object in passing. (For best results, don't deliberately "misplace" objects to provide artificial reasons for practicing this exercise. The opportunity is almost certain to present itself naturally.) Later, as you're lying in bed about to fall asleep, remember the feelings you had when you first noticed the displaced object. Allow yourself to experience the subtle annoyance of not having set the object right. Do not exaggerate these feelings, just allow them to surface naturally. Imagine youself getting up sometime in the middle of the night and setting the object straight.

Now that you've learned this exercise, you can practice whenever the opportunity presents itself. From time to time, you're bound to notice objects that are subtly out of place in your everyday environment. Rather than setting them straight at once, take the opportunity to leave some unfinished business tugging at your subconscious mind. The thought of completing your task as you fall asleep might trigger an OBE.

DAY 14

DAYS OF FUTURE PAST

You will conclude Week Two of the Free Flight Program with an exercise designed to alter your perception of time. Begin by closing your eyes and entering a state of alert relaxation. Once you are deeply relaxed, imagine yourself going about the activities that you plan for the rest of your day. Don't just rush through your planned schedule, but rather, concentrate on specific mental images of exactly where you will be, how you'll be feeling, and what you'll be perceiving at various points in your upcoming day; take the time to make these details as vivid as possible.

Look over your shoulder in your mind's eye, and observe your firsthand experiences exactly as they will occur in the near future. Try to envision even those details you might not consciously notice when the events actually take place. After you have mentally previewed your planned activities for the coming day, take a deep breath and notice the feelings in your body. Wiggle your fingers and toes, then open your eyes and begin going about your day.

As you follow through on your day's activities, remember the images you had earlier, when your body was deeply relaxed. Since the future you imagined is now occurring, you may pretend that your past self is there with you, looking over your shoulder and observing your activities. When you find yourself in a comfortable position to do so, pause in the midst of your activities and imagine that you are floating in the air behind yourself. Ask yourself if you are really where you seem to be at the moment, or if you might still be imagining things. Ask yourself if you might even be having an OBE.

Take a deep breath and, if only for an instant, imagine switching places with your past self. Then flash back into your present reality, continuing with your day as before.

You may carry this exercise further still by imagining that your present self and your future self may literally coexist. For instance, as you leave your house in the morning, imagine that you see your future self passing you on the street. Finally, take a deep breath and imagine that you're trading places with your future self. Then allow yourself to "pop" back into the present and continue with your day.

Flight Directive—Please practice the second phase of this exercise for several hours. Then take a break for two or three hours and carry out some distracting physical activity. When you've gotten enough physical exercise, enjoy the best that mundane reality and your personal relationships have to offer, just as you did at the close of Week One. You have just completed Week Two of the Free Flight Program.

WEEK TWO ROUNDUP TAKING OFF

DAY 8 RISING ABOVE IT		**DAY 9** A ROOM WITH A VIEW	**DAY 10** BEING THERE	
Enter a state of alert relaxation. Imagine your consciousness shrinking and expanding within your physical form. Imagine floating above your own body. Shift your focus of attention back and forth between your body and the point above. Imagine floating above your body for several minutes without straining. Break for an hour and repeat.	Imagine yourself floating above your body as you fall asleep at the end of the day.	Enter a state of alert relaxation. Imagine your consciousness leaving your body and crossing the room. Shift your attention back to your body. Imagine yourself floating above your body as you fall asleep at the end of the day.	Choose a meaningful indoor location. Go to a comfortable outdoor location nearby. Close your eyes and imagine that you are having an OBE; while in the midst of this imagined OBE, see yourself returning home. Still imagining that you are in the midst of an OBE, go to the meaningful indoor location you have chosen. Observe the indoor location as if you are a ghost.	

	DAY 11 SHOPPING SPREE		**DAY 12** WITHIN YOU AND WITHOUT YOU
Return to the outdoor site and while there, imagine that you are home. Go home. Enter a state of alert relaxation, and imagine that you are back at the meaningful indoor locale. Resume a state of alert waking consciousness. Imagine yourself floating above your body as you fall asleep at night.	Go to a department store or shopping center. Explore a variety of objects. Take a twenty-minute break. Return to browse through a different section of the shopping environment. Choose and buy a small gift for a special person in your life. After you leave the store, study your purchase. Take a short break.	Explore your home and the emotionally significant objects within. Enter a state of alert relaxation. Imagine yourself shrinking and floating in front of the gift you bought. Imagine yourself floating in front of one of the significant objects in your home. Imagine yourself assuming normal size and return to a state of alert waking consciousness. As you fall asleep at the end of the day, remember all the objects and imagine yourself floating above your body.	Before you get out of bed, envision your face looking back at you from above. Imagine yourself floating in front of one of the objects in your home. Envision your face again, then open your eyes and get out of bed. As you fall asleep at night, remember all the objects in your home and imagine yourself floating above your body. *(continued)*

WEEK TWO ROUNDUP TAKING OFF (continued)

DAY 13 UNFINISHED BUSINESS	**DAY 14** DAYS OF FUTURE PAST	
Before you get out of bed, envision your face looking back at you from above. Then get up. Notice the objects you often take for granted around you. Notice an object that seems crooked or out of place. Do not set it right. As you go to bed, imagine yourself setting the object right sometime during the night. Then see your face floating above you and fall asleep.	Before you get out of bed, envision your face looking back at you from above. Then open your eyes and get up. Enter a state of alert relaxation. Envision the things you will do during the day ahead. Get up and go about your day. As you go about your day, remember the images you had earlier and pretend your past self is with you now.	Imagine switching places with your past self, then flash back to present reality and continue with your day. As you go to sleep at night, imagine your face floating in the air above you.

WEEK THREE

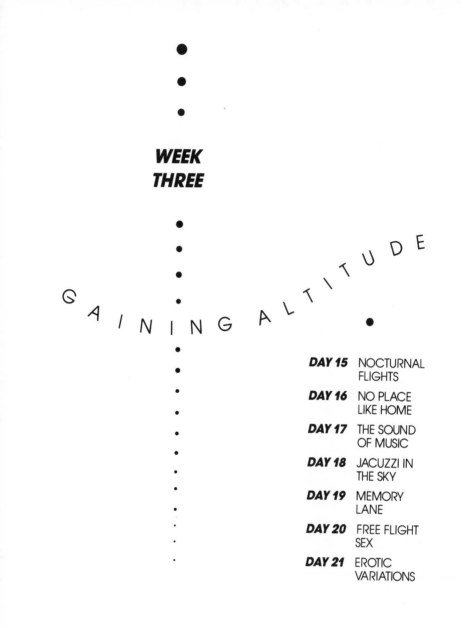

GAINING ALTITUDE

WEEK THREE

•

GAINING ALTITUDE

Week Three exercises will help you to induce OBEs in a greater variety of circumstances. You will learn how to induce spontaneous out-of-body experiences while on the verge of falling asleep or waking up. You'll also learn how to share your OBEs with a partner. Finally, we will instruct you in one of the more stimulating facets of our program: erotic out-of-body experiences, including OBE sex.

Before beginning Week Three, take a few moments to consider what you feel OBEs *should* be like. How have these expectations influenced your interpretation of your personal experience in the Free Flight Program thus far? Is it possible that you have had an OBE without even realizing it? If, after all you've gone through, you still harbor the popular notion that OBEs necessarily involve such fanciful elements as silver cords, astral bodies, discarnate entities, or other planes of existence, you may be missing the real thing.

In other words, your expectations about the experience should be realistic and not exaggerated. The Free Flight Program can open new vistas of experience for you, but you will be more likely to have these experiences if you simply let them flow. You will discover what these experiences mean *to you* if you explore them on your own terms, without imposing interpretations from mystical belief systems, the occult, or anecdotal reports. If you don't constrain yourself with rigid expectations, you may find your own OBEs characterized by features that are totally unique and new.

By the time you have reached Week Three, you may be wondering whether you have made suitable progress. If you have had an out-of-body experience at any point during the Free Flight Program, this question will no doubt have already answered itself. If you have not yet had an OBE, rest assured that you are still making progress in the program just by continuing to carry out the various exercises as described.

Whether or not you have had a full-blown out-of-body experience going into Week Three, the exercises that follow should make you feel far more comfortable with seeking out and exploring new and different psychological points of view. They can also help you take those new and different points of view to the limit—to the realm of the OBE.

DAY 15

NOCTURNAL FLIGHTS

On Day 15 of the Free Flight Program, you'll learn how to induce OBEs while falling asleep. Begin by visiting a museum or other public exhibit that elicits strong sensations and positive emotions. The site you select may be familiar, but it should not be someplace you have used for any other Free Flight exercises. The Museum of Natural History in New York City would be an ideal place to carry out this phase of the exercise, as would any art museum, botanical garden, or planetarium.

Spend at least two or three hours immersed in the environment you've chosen. Enjoy yourself. Forget about any outside concerns and simply appreciate the exhibits. Before leaving, buy some small souvenirs or postcards that will later help remind you of the feelings you had as you toured the exhibits. Place these items near your bedside before turning in for the night.

Begin practicing the next phase of this exercise just after you go to bed. As you're nodding off, clear your mind and casually give yourself permission to have an OBE sometime during the night. You may, for example, repeat the following sentence in your mind: "I'll allow myself to have an out-of-body experience."

Don't tell yourself you're going to try to have an OBE, since we only *try* to do things we believe we may not be able to accomplish. Simply allow your conscious mind to express your openness to the idea of having an OBE. Clear your mind of all other thoughts in the moment that you give yourself this permission, then let go of the thought.

Keep things simple and positive. Focus on having an OBE sometime in the future, when your unconscious mind decides it is appropriate for you to do so—tonight or any other time your inner self feels ready to enjoy the experience. As soon as you've done this, allow your thoughts to drift into pleasant recollections of the time you spent touring the exhibits you visited earlier in the day.

Depending on your personal predisposition, this technique may lead to many different types of spontaneous OBEs. For example, you may simply find yourself feeling as though you were waking up and getting out of bed sometime during the night, only to look back and notice your body still lying in bed. Conversely, you may find yourself having a vivid dream that gradually or suddenly transforms itself into an OBE. If you're prone to lucid dreaming, in which you're aware of having a dream while the dream is in progress, you may also try a variation of this exercise by giving yourself permission to have an OBE sometime during the course of one of these dreams.

If you like, as you're falling asleep, you may also give yourself permission to mentally "return" to the exhibits you explored earlier in the day.

Once you have learned the Nocturnal Flight exercise, it should become a permanent part of your OBE repertoire. Each night before you drift off to sleep, give yourself permission to have an OBE. Do the same whenever you momentarily wake up in the middle of the night. The technique is so simple that it can also be practiced during alert relaxation, and with any of the other imagery techniques you've learned over the past two weeks.

Flight Directive—Please read instructions for Day 16 before falling asleep.

DAY 16

NO PLACE LIKE HOME

Giving yourself permission to have an OBE as you're falling asleep can be particularly effective when combined with additional psychological exercises, such as the one below. Begin this exercise the first thing in the morning, while you're lying in bed. When you begin to notice yourself waking up, continue lying in bed with your eyes closed and don't move. (If you usually awaken with the assistance of an alarm clock or barks from the neighborhood dog, we suggest that you make some more subtle arrangements for getting up this morning, such as using a clock radio to awaken you to soft music.)

As you're waking up, take a few moments to feel your bed beneath you; notice the morning sounds and the smells of the surrounding room. Feel the comfortable emotional ambiance that lets you know you're waking up in familiar surroundings. Take a deep breath and open your eyes. Then take a few moments to look around the room before getting up and going about your day.

For the next part of this exercise, pick out an unusual place to spend the night: the living room sofa, the bathtub, or the kitchen floor will do. For an even more dramatic variation, try sleeping at a friend's house or renting a motel room for the night. Then, just as you find yourself on the verge of falling asleep or waking up in this unusual place, imagine that you're lying half awake in your own familiar bed, experiencing all the sensations you associate with being there.

Once you've learned this exercise, you may practice it anytime you find yourself on the verge of falling asleep or waking up in a strange environment. If you're on the road a lot or happen to be on vacaction while carrying out the Free Flight Program, this is a particularly good exercise to practice in the course of your travels. Just remember, "There's no place like home," as Dorothy would say.

As you might imagine, this same exercise may also be practiced in reverse—by imagining that you're falling asleep or waking up in some other place while you're actually lying in your own bed at home. Be creative. Don't just imagine that you're sleeping in the familiar room down the hall. How about putting yourself in an unfamiliar environment such as a room at the New York Plaza Hotel, on the White House lawn, or at the bottom of the Grand Canyon?

Imagining yourself falling asleep or waking up in a different environment can be a powerful method for inducing OBEs. This method can be even more effective when combined with the technique of gently giving yourself permission to have an OBE just as you're falling asleep.

DAY 17

THE SOUND OF MUSIC

Out-of-body experiences can take on the dimensions of whatever moods you set for them, and one of the most effective ways to modulate your state of mind is through music. In fact, for many people, listening to an emotionally stirring musical composition may be the closest they've come to having an out-of-body experience.

Since modern technology has rendered music completely

portable, you can provide yourself with a personally designed soundtrack for any type of inner experience you may feel like having, no matter where you happen to be at the time. All you need is a portable stereo, tape recorder, or CD player, a set of headphones, and appropriate music for the desired mood.

For the purpose of inducing OBEs, we recommend powerful, inspiring, uplifting classical compositions such as Handel's *Messiah,* Beethoven's *Missa Solemnis,* Mozart's Masonic Funereal Music or Grand Mass in C, Vivaldi's *Gloria,* Brahms' Requiem, or Bach's Fugue in G for Organ. If you prefer, you may use soul or modern jazz music, taping such artists as Sade and Tangerine Dream. You might also opt for electronic music of the sort played by Kitaro or Vangelis. Popular music with lots of lyrics may be distracting, though if these move you, you can use such music as well. Our own tastes in this matter lean away from most of the so-called "New Age" music, which we consider more suitable for inducing sleep than encouraging OBEs. We also discourage the use of hard rock music, which many people would find too emotionally aggressive to help them sustain a relaxed and reflective state.

> ***Flight Directive***—Before you proceed, you'll need to choose and record your music for Day 17. Since you will perform this exercise two times in the course of the day, you should choose two different pieces, each reflecting a different mood. When you make your tapes, you must be certain that each selection plays for at least an hour; obviously, this may require that you record a single composition over and over until your tape runs for the appropriate amount of time.

On Day 17, you'll practice alert relaxation in an unusual setting. You will also use different kinds of background music. Your goal: to explore the ways in which these factors influence the quality of your inner experience.

Begin by selecting a secluded but safe location dramatically different from the comfortable chair you usually use to practice alert relaxation. Try the fire escape outside your apartment window, the back yard, the front seat of your car, parked at the beach, or a pew in a local church. If you're at all nervous about doing this alone, bring a trusted friend who won't mind keeping a distance while watching over you and allowing you the necessary time to fully carry out this exercise.

When you arrive at your chosen spot, take a few moments to find an area where you'll be safe, comfortable, and undisturbed. Switch on the music, set it to an enjoyable listening level, close your eyes, and begin entering a state of alert relaxation.

As you feel yourself relaxing, imagine that you're lying back in your familiar chair where you've practiced alert relaxation in the past. Just allow this feeling to come and go without forcing it. As you become more deeply relaxed, imagine that you see your face looking back at you from above. Listen to the music playing in the background and allow yourself to flow into the feelings and emotions it stimulates in you. Imagine that you can feel yourself floating a few inches above your body.

Allow the impact of these images and feelings to evolve over the course of the next hour. For instance, imagine yourself rising far into the air above your body. Look at your surrounding environment as the music builds. Notice how your own feelings and mental images are influenced by the setting and the music. Finally, as the music moves toward its conclusion, gradually bring yourself back to a state of alert waking consciousness. Then spend at least twenty minutes relaxing in this chosen site before leaving.

Flight Directive—Take a three-hour break.

Later on, after you're back at home, play the second tape you have made and repeat the exercise in the comfort of your chair. Notice how feelings and images are powerfully induced by the music, even when you're in your everyday environment.

While practicing this exercise at home, you may also experiment by playing the same piece of music that you used earlier in the day for the first exercise. You may find the music mentally drawing you back to images of the setting where you practiced the earlier exercise. You may also find the music generating emotions similar to those you experienced at that time. You may even find that music helps to *deepen* the experience you had earlier in the day.

Flight Directive—Once you've practiced this exercise, you may want to experiment with a number of settings and many different types of music to see how they affect your inner experience, and your ability to have an OBE. Since it may not always be practical to carry a tape recorder with you, you may even want to commit at least one favorite piece of music to memory. Once you have found a selection that puts you in the ideal mood, you can "play" the piece in your imagination whenever you want.

As you continue with the Free Flight Program, you may find that playing a particular musical selection prior to an exercise or right before going to sleep can help you enter a receptive mood for inducing OBEs.

DAY 18

JACUZZI IN THE SKY

On Day 18, you'll combine several of the techniques learned in earlier exercises and practice these in a setting especially conducive to the OBE—the relaxing aquatic environment of a warm bathtub or a Jacuzzi.

If at all possible, we strongly recommend using a Jacuzzi for this exercise, since the temperature may be easily regulated and maintained, and the continuous flowing sounds and feelings of the water jets are particularly suited to the Free Flight exercises. Many communities have public facilities in which it is possible, for a nominal fee, to rent a private room with a sauna and a Jacuzzi at an hourly rate. We recommend using such a private facility for this exercise; public tubs located in your gymnasium or health club may disrupt the flow of the exercise, to say the least. If it is impossible for you to gain access to a private facility, your own bathtub at home is an acceptable alternative. Just leave the faucet slowly running to keep the water warm and circulating around you. (You may need to adjust the stopper to keep the tub from overflowing.)

Since you'll be entering a deep state of relaxation while practicing this exercise, we recommend asking a close friend to work along with you to assure that you don't overdo it or fall asleep in the tub as you're following these instructions. *It is very important that you do not carry out this exercise alone.* (It is acceptable to wear a bathing suit while conducting this exercise, if doing so makes you feel more at ease.) To keep you from risking electrocution, your friend should also operate your tape recorder. You should play the same music you used for Day 17.

Begin by setting the tub to a moderately warm temperature. (Don't set the temperature too high, since you'll remain in the water for at least thirty minutes.) Get in, stretch out, and get comfortable. Position your body so that you can completely relax without sliding down too far into the water. If you're in a Jacuzzi, turn on the jets and sit between them so that you can feel their vibration without having them pulsate directly onto your body.

Have your friend turn on the music while you close your eyes and progressively enter a state of alert relaxation. Use the warm vibrating water to help you imagine warm currents slowly moving up through your body and relaxing each of your muscles. Then, before you proceed, have your friend slowly read the instructions below, pausing momentarily where indicated.

> Subtly tell yourself, almost as a passing thought, that you are willing to have an out-of-body experience. Don't pressure yourself, just allow yourself to recognize the thought and quickly let it go as you continue relaxing. [Pause.]
>
> As you become more and more relaxed, allow your thoughts to drift into the sounds of the warm water rushing all around you and the music playing in the background. Imagine your body spreading out and becoming larger. [Pause.] Imagine your body merging with the surrounding wetness until there is no absolute distinction between you and the warm rushing water. [Pause.] Imagine your face looking

back at you from above. [Pause.] Sense your consciousness becoming lighter and lighter as your physical body feels heavier and heavier and becomes more and more deeply relaxed.

Breathe deeply; smell the moisture and feel the warmth in the air around you. Then take another deep breath and imagine yourself experiencing these same smells and feelings someplace else.

Don't try to predetermine a particular location upon which to focus your awareness. Instead, allow the feelings stirred by the music and the water to suggest a place from your deepest unconscious thoughts and memories. Allow images and feelings about this place to emerge on their own. Imagine that all the sensations you're experiencing at this moment are happening in the place that has emerged from your unconscious mind. [Pause.]

Now just let your body lie quietly, relaxing in the water, as you allow your thoughts to drift into the images and sensations of that other place.

Give yourself at least twenty minutes to enjoy this inner experience.

The reader and the OBE traveler should now be silent for twenty minutes. When the time is up, the reader should recite the following instruction:

Now gradually focus your attention back on your body and return to a state of alert waking consciousness.

Flight Directive—Rinse yourself off with cool or lukewarm water immediately following this exercise. Then lie down and rest for at least half an hour before getting up and going about any of your usual activities.

DAY 19

MEMORY LANE

On Day 19 you will become more adept than ever at conjuring distant locales. Once again, you'll combine several techniques learned in earlier exercises and practice these in a warm and relaxing aquatic environment. As with the previous day's exercise, you'll begin by practicing alert relaxation in a running bathtub or Jacuzzi. Again, we ask that you invite a close friend to look after you and help out with some of the details of this exercise.

Before you begin, think of a familiar place from your own past that you would like to concentrate on for this exercise. The location can be a room in your parents' home, your old college dorm, or any environment that you know reasonably well, as long as it gives you an intense inner experience.

> ***Flight Directive***—Many people may choose to focus on a childhood home. However, if you have unresolved feelings about your childhood, we recommend that you check with your therapist or be prepared to deal with the disturbing emotions sure to emerge. If you have any doubts about your ability to handle such an experience, simply focus on a location with more pleasant, but equally intense, psychological associations, such as a favorite beach where you once had a wonderful picnic, or a beautiful cathedral where you've gone to feel a deep sense of inner peace.

Now, think of music that reminds you of the place you have in mind. For example: If your place is the house you grew up in, what kind of music did you listen to there? If it's the building where you work, do they pipe in music over loudspeakers? If it's a cathedral, have you heard organ music played there? If you do not associate a particular kind of music with your location, what kind of music is emotionally compatible with it? When you decide on the appropriate music, make a forty-five minute tape recording of it.

Once your musical arrangements have been set up, the exercise can commence. If possible, return to the place where you practiced the Day 18 exercise. Begin by setting the water temperature to a moderately warm level, getting in, and getting comfortable. Remember to position yourself so that you can become deeply relaxed without slipping completely into the water. With your music playing in the background, close your eyes and use the warm vibrating water to help you imagine warm currents moving up through your body and relaxing all of your muscles. By now you may find that entering a state of alert relaxation is becoming easier, and that it may take much less time than it originally did for you to become very deeply relaxed. As you did on the previous day, quietly tell yourself that you are willing to have an OBE; then just let the thought go and forget about it. Imagine the edges of your body merging with the edges of the moving water.

When you have achieved this state, your companion should start to read aloud from the instructions below, substituting the name of the place you have selected whenever possible.

> Imagine that you are in the place you've selected. Imagine yourself sitting or standing there, experiencing the input of all your senses. [Pause.] What does the area smell like? [Pause.] What kind of sounds do you hear? [Pause.] What are people doing there? [Pause.] Allow yourself to experience all your emotional feelings about the place. [Pause.] Does it make you feel happy? [Pause.] Sad? [Pause.] Has anything special ever happened to you there? [Pause.] How do you feel about this environment from your present perspective? [Pause.] Think of the place upon which you are focusing not just as you remember it, but exactly as it looks and feels at this moment, allowing all the information from your emotions and senses to gradually emerge. [Pause.]
>
> Now experience the place from different and surprising perspectives. [Pause.] If you're focusing on a room, for example, allow yourself to experience it from up above, near the ceiling. [Pause.] Imagine yourself sitting in a variety of positions to achieve different points of view. [Pause.] Imagine yourself on your back on the floor looking up. [Pause.] Then experience the room upon which you've been focusing from the next room. [Pause.] Gradually move from place to place around the immediate environment, experiencing each position from continuously changing perspectives. [Pause.]
>
> Relax in the water, immersing yourself in the location upon which you've been focusing. Allow the emerging sensations to flow through your awareness without analyzing or controlling them. View your inner images as if they were scenes from a film. You have twenty minutes, and I will let you know when your time is up. But try to remember, you are in charge of your own experience. If you start to feel uncomfortable, just tune into the sounds and feelings of your body lying in the

> water. By doing so, you will instantly shift your focus back to your familiar perspective toward reality.

The reader and the OBE traveler should now be silent for twenty minutes. When the time is up, the reader should recite the following instruction:

> Now gradually focus your attention back on your body and return to alert waking consciousness.

> ***Flight Directive***—Rinse yourself off with cool or lukewarm water immediately following this exercise. Lie down and rest for at least thirty minutes to an hour before resuming your day's activities.

DAY 20

FREE FLIGHT SEX

On Day 20 you'll learn how to share your out-of-body experiences with a partner. We recommend that this exercise be practiced by two consenting adults who are accustomed to having sex with each other and sleeping together. If your personal situation renders this impossible, however, the exercise may still be carried out with a close platonic friend.

If you are accustomed to sleeping with your partner, you should sleep in separate rooms for this exercise. Be sure to synchronize your practice sessions from these two different locations. If you are not accustomed to sleeping with the partner you have chosen for this exercise, you should still synchronize your sessions with each other and follow the instructions below as far as is comfortably possible. For instance, if the sexual component of the exercise is inappropriate to your relationship, substitute an emotional union instead.

You and your partner should both begin by entering a

deeply relaxed state just prior to falling asleep. While in this state, remember the physical and sexual sensations you have when you're lying close to your partner. What relative positions do you usually take when you're lying in bed together? How does it feel to wrap your arms around your partner and press up against him or her? What is it like to slowly and very gently run your hands up and down the curves of your partner's completely naked body and feel the warmth and smoothness of your partner's skin? How does it make you feel to listen your partner breathing and feel the rhythmic motions of his or her body? How do the smells you've come to associate with your partner affect your sexual feelings toward this person? How do you react to pressure from your partner's fingers, or the moisture of your partner's tongue? Where do you especially like to touch and be touched by your partner? In what ways do you touch each other in those special places, and how does this make you feel, both emotionally and physically?

If your partner is in a familiar environment, such as your bedroom, you may help this exercise along by remembering the room and all its attendant sensations in as much detail as you can. If he or she is in an unfamiliar environment, just imagine your partner lying in a familiar position beside you where you are right now. Particularly, recall any emotions that remind you of being with this person, and how you feel when you're touching each other in special, sexual ways.

What sorts of things do you and your partner say to each other when you're quietly lying in bed together? How about when you're locked together in the heat of a particularly passionate lovemaking session? Though you are physically separated, speak your fantasies to each other in your minds, imagining that you can hear each other's thoughts: *Let me touch you, here. Right here. Right now.* Imagine yourself touching your partner in a special way as you speak these thoughts in your mind, feeling all the sensations you associate with this action.

Then listen to your partner's imagined response in your thoughts: *That feels soooo good.* Imagine your partner responding sexually and emotionally to your thoughts of touching and caressing. Then imagine your partner touching you, again "hearing" his or her words in your mind: *I can feel you getting excited. It turns me on when you get turned on. Oh, this is great.*

Remember the way you feel when your partner touches you in a special way. Imagine yourself feeling those same sensations at this very moment.

If you are not accustomed to having sex with your partner, simply focus on the physical and emotional feelings you do have when in his or her physical presence and imagine yourself experiencing these same feelings now at a distance. You may maintain this inner experience for a period of time previously agreed upon with your partner or for as long as this feels comfortable to you.

You and your partner may follow this exercise as far as your imagination comfortably allows—the perfect culmination, of course, would be imagining yourselves having sexual intercourse with each other from a physical distance. Initially, the result may be little more than a sense of shared camaraderie, communication, or remembered sexuality, or simply a shared sense of closeness at a distance. Whether in this initial session or in subsequent sessions, the result may also be a mutual OBE that adds a wonderful new dimension to your sexual and emotional relationship.

This exercise can be practiced whenever you and your partner find yourselves physically separated. It may be practiced while you and your partner are falling asleep or while you are both in a state of alert relaxation. If you both agree to do so, you can even experiment by practicing this exercise without synchronizing your sessions in advance. You may find it useful to prepare independent descriptions of your individual experiences so you can later compare notes.

DAY 21

EROTIC VARIATIONS

Today you will practice an advanced form of the shared OBE exercise. As with Day 20, you and your partner should deliberately sleep in different beds, preferably in separate rooms or buildings from each other. Before you and your partner separate, however, you should take a candle-light bath or a shower together, then spend at least one or two hours taking turns massaging each other all over with warm, scented oil, kissing, touching, and holding each other, and passionately making love. You might also enhance the atmosphere by lighting candles and burning incense in the room where you're having sex. Pretend you've just met, and that you're discovering each other sexually for the first time. Think about those aspects of your partner's sexuality that most attracted and excited you when you first got together, and that most strongly affect you now. Use this experience as an opportunity to completely enjoy and connect with each other on a physical, emotional, and spiritual level, forgetting for the time being about any outside concerns that may be on your minds.

Pick out some favorite sexual thing to do, such as slowly stroking your partner into increasingly powerful multiple orgasms, or tickling your partner lightly all over with a feather or clean paintbrush. Then think of some equally exciting thing for your partner to do to you, such as covering your sexual organs with chocolate sauce or warm orange marmalade or steak juice and slowly licking it off, rubbing small ice cubes lightly over your nipples, or teasing you with colorful silk scarves. If making a sexual connection isn't possible or comfortable with your partner, your actions should still be as affectionate as possible—kiss each other, hug each other, or even hold hands.

You should then part, spending the night in physically

separate locations, and agree to think about your most recent sexual-emotional experiences together at designated times while you're both either falling asleep or deep in a state of alert relaxation. As you did on Day 20, remember the physical and sexual sensations you had when you were with your partner, imagining that you are still connecting with each other on a deep, inner level at this moment.

Once again, carefully synchronize your practice sessions from your two different locations and, as much as possible, take notes about your feelings and experiences. Begin by entering a deeply relaxed state and remembering the way it feels to be with your partner. Do you associate any special smells with this person? Remember the smell of your partner's laundry detergent, clothing, cologne or perfume, and especially the scent of the massage oil you used in the earlier part of this exercise when the two of you were together.

Remember all the physical sensations you associate with your partner. Concentrate, also, on how you feel emotionally when you think of this person. If your partner is in your bedroom, think about the room. Where is the furniture placed? How is the room arranged? Remember the room in as much detail as you can, especially recalling the way it looked and felt while you and your partner were making love. If your partner is in an unfamiliar environment, imagine him or her in a familiar position beside you, where you are right now.

Think about your partner, what he or she looks like, the sound of his or her voice, the feeling of his or her naked body pressing against yours. Remember the special sexual things you did together in the earlier part of the exercise. What did that feel like? For you? Between the two of you? Think of your partner now, doing what he or she was doing to you earlier. Think of yourself, also doing in this moment whatever you did to your partner then. Now think about doing something surprising to mentally connect with your partner. Imagine yourself kissing him or her in some particularly sexy and affectionate place, lightly stroking his or her sexual organs, or caressing the soft curves of his or her completely naked body.

Imagine yourself listening to your partner breathing; imagine your partner's breathing pattern becoming irregular and pronounced as the two of you make love. Notice the way your own breathing pattern changes as you consider the sexual thoughts and feelings your partner is having about you *right now.*

Once again, speak your thoughts and fantasies to your partner in your mind. *Move this way, so I can touch you right there, right now.* Imagine yourself gently touching your partner's sexual organs as you speak these thoughts in your mind. Feel your partner respond to your touch.

Listen to your partner's imagined reply: *Higher, longer, don't stop.* Imagine your partner getting more and more excited at the feel of your touch. Then imagine your partner touching you in a similar sexual fashion at the same time, saying to you, *And I'm touching you here. And here. And here.*

Remember the feelings you have when your partner touches you sexually, and imagine yourself feeling those same sensations now. Say to your partner, in your thoughts, *I love that. Touch me just like that, right there, while I'm touching you.* Continue imagining yourself communicating and having sexual relations with your partner in this fashion, slowly building up to a point where you can imagine yourselves experiencing sexual intercourse together from a distance.

Again, if you are not used to having sex with your partner, concentrate instead on the physical and emotional feelings you do have when you're with this person and imagine yourselves sharing that sense of each other's physical presence from a distance. As before, you may continue exploring this inner experience for a prearranged period of time, or for as long as you feel comfortable doing so.

As on Day 20, the initial result of this exercise may be little more than a wild sexual fantasy. However, with repeated practice in conjunction with the rest of the Free Flight exercises, it can lead to a full-blown, mutual OBE. Since this exercise may be practiced whenever you and your partner find it necessary to be physically apart, it may be one way for the two of you to maintain a sense of communication and shared sexuality.

Whether you and your partner are conducting this exercise

while one or both of you are falling asleep or in a state of alert relaxation, we strongly encourage you to remember your experiences and compare notes at a later date. You may also enjoy reinforcing these mental experiences by reenacting them in exquisite detail the next time you're together again.

Flight Directive—After practicing this exercise, perhaps you and your partner will want to do something special with each other, like going out to dinner and a movie, going for a walk in the park, or making wild, passionate love once again in person. It's time to celebrate! After all, you have not only just made a very special connection, you have also completed Week Three of the Free Flight Program.

WEEK THREE ROUNDUP GAINING ALTITUDE

DAY 15 NOCTURNAL FLIGHTS	**DAY 16** NO PLACE LIKE HOME	**DAY 17** THE SOUND OF MUSIC	
Before you get out of bed, envision your face looking back at you from above. Then open your eyes and get up. Visit a museum or other public exhibit. Enjoy yourself for a couple of hours. After you go to bed, give yourself permission to have an OBE. Then think about the exhibit and see your face floating above you. Finally fall asleep.	Before you get out of bed, envision your face looking back at you from above. Then open your eyes and get up. Pick an unusual place to spend the night. While on the verge of falling asleep, imagine that you are in your own, familiar, bed. Give yourself permission to have an OBE. Then see your face floating above you, and fall asleep.	Before you get out of bed in this strange environment, imagine that you are at home in your own, familiar bed. Then envision your face looking back at you from above. Finally, open your eyes and get up. Choose two different musical compositions representing two different moods and make an hour-long tape of each, taping each piece as many times as necessary. Choose a safe, secluded, and dramatic location away from home.	Go to that location, turn on the music, and enter a state of alert relaxation. Imagine that you are back at home, in the very spot you usually use to enter alert relaxation. Listen to the music and see your face looking back at you from above. As the music concludes, bring yourself back to a state of alert waking consciousness. Remain at your chosen site for an additional twenty mintues before leaving.

	DAY 18 JACUZZI IN THE SKY		**DAY 19** MEMORY LANE
Take a three-hour break. Later, back at home, repeat the exercise with the second tape you have made. While on the verge of falling asleep, give yourself permission to have an OBE. See your face floating above you, and fall asleep.	Before you get out of bed, envision your face looking back at you from above. Then open your eyes and get up. Recruit the aid of a close friend and then locate a private hot tub or prepare your own bathtub with warm water. Enter a state of alert relaxation as your friend plays the same music you listened to on Day 17. Listen to the instructions beginning on page 51, as read by your friend.	Imagine your body spreading out to become one with the water. Imagine that you are someplace else. Focus on the images of this other place for twenty minutes. Return to a state of alert waking consciousness. Rest for thirty minutes before continuing with your day. While on the verge of falling asleep at night, give yourself permission to have an OBE. Then see your face floating above you, and fall asleep.	Before you get out of bed, envision your face looking back at you from above. Then open your eyes and get up. Choose a familiar place from your own past that you would like to focus on. Choose a musical composition, or series of compositions, that reminds you of that location, and make a forty-five minute audio tape. Return with your friend to the hot tub or bathtub you used yesterday. *(continued)*

WEEK THREE ROUNDUP GAINING ALTITUDE (continued)

DAY 19 MEMORY LANE	**DAY 20** FREE FLIGHT SEX		**DAY 21** EROTIC VARIATIONS
As your friend plays the music, enter a state of alert relaxation. Envision yourself in the meaningful locale from the past for at least twenty minutes as your companion reads aloud the instructions beginning on page 53. Return to alert waking consciousness and rest for thirty minutes before continuing with your day. While on the verge of falling asleep, give yourself permission to have an OBE. Then see your face floating above you, and fall asleep.	Before you get out of bed, envision your face looking back at you from above. Then open your eyes and get up. Choose a partner, preferably a lover you are close to. If this is not possible, however, ask a close platonic friend to participate. Make sure that you and your partner spend this night in separate locations. Prior to falling asleep, both you and your partner must enter a state of alert relaxation.	Both should review the physical or emotional feelings experienced when together. While on the verge of falling asleep, give yourself permission to have an OBE. Then see your face floating above you, and fall asleep.	Before you get out of bed, envision your face looking back at you from above. Then open your eyes and get up. Sometime during the day, have an intimate sexual or emotional encounter with your partner. Just like yesterday, you and your partner must sleep in different beds. Enter a state of alert relaxation, and remember the physical or emotional encounter you had earlier in the day.

Imagine a new sexual or emotional encounter, and act it out in your mind. Imagine that you and your partner are actually in the midst of this encounter, right now.

While on the verge of falling asleep, give yourself permission to have an OBE. Then imagine your partner, see your face floating above you, and fall asleep.

WEEK FOUR

FLYING

WEEK FOUR

•

F L Y I N G

During Week Four, you will learn the most advanced Free Flight techniques, tapping such potent boosters as sleep deprivation, orgasm, and shifts in your perception of time. You will also understand our techniques well enough to develop your own ongoing personalized approach. Indeed, by the time you have reached Day 30, you should be able to custom-design your Free Flight travels just as some people custom-design their homes, clothes, and cars.

Once you can induce a diversity of "designer" OBEs, you will understand what only the initiated can: there are many types of OBEs corresponding to a wide range of emotions and perspectives. OBEs may vary in their degree of intensity, creating sensations of separation from the physical body to a greater or lesser extent. They may vary in terms of the specific form and content. Your OBEs will probably tap a broader range of experience than everyday waking reality, and unlike waking reality, the only limitation to the OBE may be your imagination itself.

Despite this fact, during Week Four you will be able to test the *objective* reality of your OBEs as well. By performing some informal experiments based on work done at Duke University, the Institute for Advanced Psychology, and elsewhere, you will be able to explore the notion that some or all aspects of your OBE travels are literally *real*.

As you complete the Free Flight Program, remember to keep a balanced perspective; if you do so, your inner journeys will aid, not impede, your interaction with external reality. As you become more expert, your Free Flight experiences should certainly help you achieve new perspectives on your relationship with other people and the outside world.

DAY 22

THE NIGHT WATCH

For those who crave particularly intense and prolonged versions of the OBE, sleep deprivation may be the key. You will start to lay the groundwork for this route to altered consciousness on Day 22.

> ***Flight Directive***—You must be both psychologically and physically stable to carry out this exercise. If you have any doubts, check with your doctor or therapist. Even if you *are* perfectly healthy, work or other commitments might make it impractical for you to go without sleep at this time. If so, spend Days 22 and 23 reviewing earlier exercises; practice sleep deprivation only when your schedule safely permits.

Your preparation for at least twenty-four hours of sleep deprivation begins early in the morning of Day 22. Before getting out of bed, moving, or even opening your eyes, imagine your face looking back at you from above. Take your time and allow this image to fully form. Then imagine that you're floating in the air just above your body. Focus all your senses on the space around you, and imagine that you're looking down on your body lying below you on the bed. Maintain this focus for at least twenty or thirty minutes. Then gradually bring yourself into a state of full waking consciousness. Wiggle your fingers and toes, and get up and go about your day's activities.

Conserve your energy as much as possible throughout the day by eating lightly and avoiding any overly strenuous activities. Whenever it occurs to you, affirm the thought that you're open to having an out-of-body experience sometime in the future. Then, as soon as the thought passes through your mind, let it go. Remember that it's important not to pressure yourself, but only to acknowledge and recognize your innermost feelings.

Go about your usual daily routine in every other way. Then, later, during the time when you would normally be asleep, choose some low-key activities such as listening to music, watching movie videos, or reading a book.

As the night wears on, you may notice that the passage of time seems to shift its dimensions. A few hours of relative solitude in the middle of the night may seem to pass more quickly or slowly than the same number of hours in the social and working reality of mid-afternoon.

You may also notice that sleep deprivation can induce a state of intense objectivity, in which you may feel as though you are observing your own thoughts and experiences from a distance. It may even seem as if you're watching yourself act out the role of the main character in a late night movie about your life. This state of awareness can make you feel less "locked into" your body. It can also alter your perception of reality, sometimes so dramatically that you feel somehow disconnected from the ordinary world. Immerse yourself in this sense of separation as the night goes on.

Open the window and gaze at the surrounding darkness. Breathe in deeply and imagine that you're inhaling a part of the night. Then release your breath, pushing a deep inner part of yourself back out into the dark and quiet of the night. Allow yourself to feel a sense of connection with the rest of humanity and the natural world. Give yourself time to reflect on the experience of being alive, and on what this experience means to you on a deeply personal level. Then close the window and continue to sit quietly while remaining awake.

When the night begins edging closer to the morning, open the window again and watch the dark sky gradually become saturated with sunlight. Notice signs of life: lights coming on in nearby houses, moving cars, and people or animals walking about outside.

DAY 23

THE MORNING AFTER

On Day 23 you'll continue with the next phase of the sleep deprivation exercise you began last night. First, see how you feel. If you're feeling at all ill or uneasy by morning, terminate the exercise here. To do so, go straight to bed, and as you're falling asleep tell yourself that you may have an out-of-body experience sometime before you wake up.

If you feel fine, however, you may want to intensify your Free Flight potential in the following way: after you've been awake for roughly twenty-four hours, after the sun comes up and you feel it's safe to walk around outside, fix yourself a light breakfast and then go out for an easygoing walk. Stay out no more than twenty or thirty minutes, and make sure you're no more than fifteen minutes from your home at any given moment. While walking, tune into your surroundings and note how they may seem different than usual. Notice the smell and temperature of the air, and even subtle sounds such as the call of an early morning bird or the soft whirr of a neighbor's car being driven to work.

When you return home, immediately kick off your shoes. Put on some relaxing background music, lie down on the sofa or in a comfortable chair and slowly enter a state of alert relaxation. Pay particular attention to the need to remain awake and alert as you enter a deeply relaxed state. Picture your own face looking directly back at you from above, and imagine yourself floating in the air above your body.

Remember the feelings and impressions you had a short while ago as you walked near your home. Imagine that you are back out there, this time floating above the ground. First experience the environment as it was a short while ago. Then experience it as you believe it must be right now. Give yourself at least fifteen minutes to enjoy these impressions while you remain as alert and relaxed as possible. Then reaffirm your willingness to have an out-of-body experience, and allow yourself to drift off to sleep.

If you are in good health and can comfortably handle it, you may heighten your OBE still further by depriving yourself of yet more sleep. This may be accomplished either by staying awake as much beyond the twenty-four-hour period as you can or by gradually reducing the amount of sleep you get over several nights, so that at the end of a week or two you're much more sleep-deprived than usual. Use your judgment, and when warranted check with your doctor or therapist to see if sleep deprivation could possibly put you at risk.

> ***Flight Directive***—After you've completed the sleep deprivation exercise, spend the day relaxing and catching up on your rest. Later on in the evening, when you are going to sleep for the night, practice the presleep techniques you learned on Day 15.

DAY 24

ORGASMIC FLIGHTS

The exercises for Day 24 are purely sexual. In them, you will learn how to enter the realm of the out-of-body experience through the orgasm, a very intense, highly sensitized and focused yet deeply expansive state of being. More likely than not, the orgasmic experience has had a profound effect on your self-image and your life. Now it can propel you to have an OBE.

The following exercises may be done with a partner or alone. If you feel uncomfortable with what we've suggested here, it's perfectly acceptable to use today as an opportunity to review any of the previous Free Flight exercises. We suggest that you carefully review today's exercises before you practice them so that you won't have to interrupt your sexual experiences to refer to these instructions.

Begin the exercises for Day 24 by reflecting on your own sexuality, and thinking about sex and orgasm. Think about this carefully and in great detail. Remember the events leading up to the last time you had an orgasm, your state of mind at the time, and your thoughts before it happened, as it was happening, and right afterward.

If you are alone, focus on the kinds of actions, feelings, and erotic images that you find most sexually stimulating. Put on some romantic music, or a sexy movie, and wear some perfume or cologne. Pour yourself a nice glass of wine or cranberry juice and find a place to get comfortable. Think about the last time you made love with someone special, and how that was for both of you at the height of erotic passion. Imagine yourself slowly undressing the person of your wildest, most private sexual fantasies, caressing your lover's naked body, and touching your lover in special ways. Then imagine this person slowly undressing you and taking you to a romantically stimulating place, such as a private swimming pool, a clearing in a redwood forest, or a moonlit seashore, and doing everything with you that you've ever secretly wanted a lover to do. Take your time and enjoy the fantasy. Relax. Whenever you feel comfortable, allow yourself to have an orgasm. Enjoy the experience as completely as possible without analyzing or resisting it.

If you are with a partner, take some time to make yourself look especially attractive—dress up in sexy clothes, and wear some nice perfume or cologne. Put on some romantic music and pour a glass of wine or cranberry juice for each of you. Then find someplace comfortable to relax together and make love.

Instead of rushing into it, take some time to talk about your fantasies of what you would like to do to your partner, and what you would most enjoy having your partner do to you. Be specific, allowing any sense of surprise or embarrassment this may stimulate in you to heighten your sense of sexual arousal.

Don't just tell your partner, *I want you to make love with me*. Instead, say something like, *I want you to slowly kiss my breasts all over,* or, *I'm going to put my hand in your pants and not let go or stop touching you until I feel you letting go first.* Then slowly undress each other, pretending you're discovering each other sexually for the first time. Fulfill the fantasies the two of you just talked about, eventually having sexual intercourse and allowing yourselves to have orgasms.

Whether you are enjoying this exercise on your own or with a partner, when it feels comfortable for you to do so again, either shortly after your first release or later in the same day, repeat the experience—have another orgasm—only this time, while it's happening, try to be as consciously aware of your innermost feelings as possible.

Then think about the orgasm you just had. How did it feel? Was it powerful? Did it make you feel powerful? What were you thinking about while it was happening? Pay attention to all of your emotional and physical feelings.

When you feel physically and emotionally distanced from the previous exercise, envision outer space: the fringes of the solar system, the rings of Saturn, the surface of the Moon, or anyplace else in the cosmos you might like to "visit" in an OBE. Tell yourself that during your next orgasm you're going to visit that location in your mind. Once you've selected a cosmic locale, allow yourself to experience another orgasm. Concentrate on your images of and feelings about the place you've selected before, during, and after your sexual release.

> ***Flight Directive***—If you're unable to "make it" to your cosmic goal, do not be discouraged. You may repeat the exercise as many times as you wish, and getting there is at least half the fun. By the way, even if you don't end up "visiting" the locale of your choice, this exercise may still induce an OBE.

If you're working with a partner, here's another exercise you can practice as well. Jointly choose a place to "visit" during an OBE. Then focus on reaching orgasm together as you mentally visit the place you've chosen. Imagine the two of you, joined in a moment of passion, floating together in outer space and looking back at the Earth from a distance. Maintain your mental images while focusing on your sexual and emotional feelings for as long as is comfortably possible. Imagine yourselves communicating with each other in your thoughts during this experience:

> I'm with you here, now.
>
> I feel you with me on every level, over every inch of my body, and inside it too.

If you don't achieve the desired state the first time you practice this exercise, don't be concerned or put pressure on yourself or your partner. You may find it enjoyable to just repeat the exercise on a regular basis and allow it to evolve over time.

DAY 25

TIME TRAVEL

By this point in the Free Flight Program you probably recognize that OBEs are not subject to the same spatial or temporal limitations as everyday waking reality. You may therefore, at any point, determine to "visit" places at increasingly greater distances from your body. You may also focus your awareness on the distant past or future.

Day 25 will be devoted to the mental experience of time travel. Begin by entering a state of alert relaxation. Imagine your face looking back at you from above. Now focus on the time and place you're interested in "visiting."

First try focusing your thoughts on the distant past, choosing a time and place you find personally or historically interesting. You may, for example, decide to focus on prehistoric times, when dinosaurs roamed the Earth.

To accomplish this, take a deep breath and imagine yourself floating in the air above a prehistoric lake in California. It isn't necessary to imagine yourself traveling backward year by year through time, or traveling across the physical distance separating you from the place you've chosen. Instead, just imagine your present surroundings dissolving and being replaced by that distant place and time.

Take a deep breath and imagine the smell of dinosaurs and giant ferns. Listen for the grunts and chewing sounds of a brontosaurus munching on lakeside vegetation, or the roar of the vicious allosaurus looking for some unsuspecting lunch. Imagine yourself moving through the lush vegetation, feeling sticky leaves brush against you as tiny rodentlike mammals hide beneath your feet. Feel the heat and humidity, and allow yourself to smell volcanic ash blowing in the air. After a while your experience may begin to feel less deliberately structured, more spontaneous and surprising. You may see things that you didn't consciously expect, such as dinosaurs that appear different than the ways they've been depicted in books and museums. At that point you may subjectively feel as though you are actually back in prehistoric times, exploring your OBE environment with all of your senses.

In another example, you may decide to focus on ancient Egypt during the building of the Pyramids. To accomplish this, take a deep breath and imagine yourself appearing in the air above the Egyptian desert as your present physical surroundings dissolve in your awareness. Imagine yourself smelling the dry heat of the desert air. Listen for the sounds of heavy stones being dragged across the sand by thousands of workers. Focus on the mysterious face of the Sphinx, and imagine yourself looking directly into it while floating above the sand. Continue directing your attention toward impressions and images you associate with ancient Egypt and the Pyramids, until your inner experience becomes more and more spontaneous and you subjectively feel as though you're actually there.

Don't be concerned if your awareness seems to fluctuate between your present physical surroundings and the place and time upon which you're focusing your innermost attention. Just focus as much of your attention as is comfortably possible on your mental journey, without pressuring yourself to make your inner experience any more intense than it naturally becomes on its own. As you may by now have realized, with practice your mental journeys are likely to become more intense and can naturally evolve into full-blown out-of-body experiences.

Sustain your mental sojourn for at least twenty or thirty minutes. Allow your mind to roam freely around the time and place you've chosen, and experience it from a wide variety of perspectives. Then, without bringing yourself back to a state of full waking consciousness, deliberately shift your focus of attention to a place and time in the far distant future.

As with the earlier part of this exercise, the future setting you choose should be as dramatically interesting as possible. You might focus on what your present surroundings will be like in three hundred years; or you may envision the planet Earth as seen from the surface of the Moon three thousand years in the future. Maintain this focus for at least twenty or thirty minutes before shifting your attention completely back to your body and your present physical surroundings. Wiggle your fingers and toes, feel the area immediately beneath and around your body, open your eyes, and look around the room. Allow yourself to feel completely grounded in everyday reality before getting up and going about the rest of your day's activities.

A variation on Free Flight time travel may be practiced whenever you find yourself in an historically interesting environment. One of our participants, for example, practiced this exercise while relaxing between the upright stones of Stonehenge. Yet another carried out the exercise while sitting in a gazebo not far from the senate in the ruins of ancient Rome. In both cases, the images and experiences that resulted were subjectively profound and startling, and were more intense than might be expected when focusing upon the same locations from a greater distance.

To practice this form of time travel, position yourself at some central point in the modern-day site of the historical location you've chosen. Close your eyes, and enter a state of alert relaxation. Meanwhile, imagine your surroundings dissolving in a mist, to be replaced by the same surroundings at some remote point in the past. Take your time and allow your feelings and impressions to gradually emerge. Once your impressions have solidified, shift your spatial perspective in any way that feels comfortable. If you feel at ease in this location, you may focus your attention on the same site at some point in the far distant future as well.

DAY 26

METAMORPHOSIS

Have you ever wanted to be Cleopatra? Or Lassie? Or an alien from outer space? If so, the following exercise is for you. On Day 26, you'll learn how to have OBEs in which you may assume a variety of animal, human, and other forms. Begin by spending part of your day at the local park, zoo, or aquarium. Focus your attention on the animals themselves. It isn't necessary to observe all of the animals in the place you've chosen, only to spend some time observing those for which you feel a special affinity.

When you've found an individual animal with which you feel particularly empathetic, calmly focus all of your attention on it for twenty or thirty minutes. Compare your own personality with the attributes you discern in the animal. Imagine what it would be like to experience reality from the animal's perspective. Sit quietly, relax, take a deep breath, and imagine yourself, if only for an instant, mentally switching places with the animal you're observing. Imagine the animal's physical form replacing your own body. Look into the animal's eyes and imagine that the animal's face is your own face looking back at you. Then distance yourself from the animal, and concentrate on the attributes that make you very different from each other.

Return home, or find a comfortable nearby location, and enter a state of alert relaxation. We suggest that you bring along a friend to slowly read you the following instructions, so that you may proceed with the rest of the exercise without interruption. You may also tape these instructions or commit them to memory so you can practice on your own.

As you begin to relax, remember the animal you focused on earlier. Close your eyes and imagine the animal's face looking back at you. Now imagine that the animal's face is really your own. Imagine yourself taking the form of the animal and existing in an environment appropriate to your new species. Experience the smells, sounds, and feelings of this environment in your animal form.

Now envision yourself in your animal environment looking up into the air. Imagine that you can observe a pale blue bubble of light floating in the air immediately above you. Take a deep breath and focus all of your attention on the floating bubble. Now imagine your consciousness entering the bubble from the animal below. Imagine the edges of the bubble defining the edges of your form. Imagine yourself floating in the air observing the environment and animal below you.

Take another deep breath and imagine the bubble floating in the air above your own, human body. Then imagine the bubble merging with your body as it touches down. Take another deep breath and experience yourself back "in" your body. Open your eyes, wiggle your fingers and toes, and bring yourself back to waking reality.

Flight Directive—As this exercise suggests, you may experience your OBEs in a wide variety of forms. As the days pass, you may practice this exercise in the mental form of a dolphin, a kangaroo, or a fragrant blooming rose. We also suggest that you explore the sensation of being a pure and formless point of awareness in space. Quite possibly this may be the purest and most unadulterated form of the OBE.

DAY 27

EXTENDED PERCEPTION

Because so many of the Free Flight exercises rely on your imagination, you may be wondering if there is any objective reality to your OBEs at all. On Days 27 and 28, you will have an opportunity to explore this issue through a series of informal experiments.

You may conduct these experiments whether you have experienced full-blown OBEs or a more rudimentary form of OBE imagery. In fact, the sessions themselves may actually help to stimulate OBEs by giving you a tangible and verifiable focus for your inner experiences.

These informal experiments are based on OBE studies carried out at Duke University and other laboratories. Back in 1973, Keith Harary joined psychologist Robert Morris and an interdisciplinary team of researchers bent on learning whether OBEs were purely imaginary or had some tangible basis in everyday reality. Harary himself was crucial to the project not only as a researcher but also because of his ability to induce his own OBEs at will. By deliberately inducing out-of-body experiences during this series of pioneering experiments, he provided his fellow researchers with the ability to carefully compare "active" experimental periods with control periods, when he did not induce OBEs.

One thing the researchers discovered was that OBEs apparently sometimes enabled Harary to glimpse distant events. For instance, during two double-blind sessions, one at Duke and the other at the American Society for Psychical Research, he was able to accurately describe complex collections of objects placed in distant laboratory rooms; in one of these experiments, the objects were placed a quarter of a mile away from his physical location. During another session, Harary drew pictures that closely resembled a lighted geometrical image displayed in a laboratory building next door.

The research team also discovered that Harary could apparently communicate from a distance during his out-of-body experiences. For instance, fellow researchers spontaneously identified the times when Harary, a quarter to a half mile away, reported having OBEs in their midst. Harary's pet cat, Spirit, also got into the act, dramatically quieting down whenever Harary reported mentally "visiting" the cat from a distant laboratory. The details of these landmark experiments have already been reported in dozens of publications, so we'll focus instead on how you may conduct your own informal research.

We strongly encourage you to seek any objective elements in your own OBEs as well. Begin, on Day 27, by asking a friend to select a group of objects you've never seen before. (The objects should bear no particular relationship to one another outside of their mutual use in this experiment. Your friend might, for example, select a cheese Danish, an ethnic newspaper, a Halloween mask, an alarm clock, a pair of panty hose, and a rubber chicken.) The friend should place these objects in a familiar and easily recognizable location; you yourself must avoid that location—and your friend—for at least an hour before you begin the experiment.

Of course, your friend might consider what you're asking a little bit unusual. You may, therefore, have to gently convince this person that you're serious and need his or her assistance. You might, for example, begin by telling your friend to "pick an odd collection of objects I've never seen and put them on your dining room table. I want to try an experiment."

Your friend might then reasonably ask, "What kind of experiment?" You can then enjoy explaining that you're going to induce an out-of-body experience, in which you'll "visit" your friend's dining room, and that you'll later try to tell him or her about what's on the table.

After your friend has set up the objects for you, find a comfortable place where you won't be disturbed and enter a state of alert relaxation. As you relax, breathe deeply and imagine your face looking back at you. Imagine the room around you gradually dissolving as you mentally visit the location where the objects have been placed.

Imagine yourself in this distant environment, and, in your mind, observe the objects there from a variety of shifting perspectives. Explore this environment for ten or fifteen minutes, calmly noticing your thoughts and impressions without pressuring yourself to identify the objects. Remember to focus not only on visual information, but also on smells, textures, and sounds. Then gradually focus your awareness on your body and present physical surroundings. As soon as you return to waking consciousness, make detailed notes and drawings; record all impressions of the objects selected by your friend.

Once you have recorded your impressions, you and your

friend should physically go to the location and examine the objects. Are there any similarities between your impressions and the objects that were actually chosen for you?

Please remember, this informal experiment is not as tightly controlled as those carried out in scientific laboratories, where objects would be chosen randomly. Therefore, it does not constitute an absolute test of the objective reality of the OBE. It is, rather, simply a means of exploring the notion that your OBEs may be objectively verifiable in some way.

DAY 28

EXTENDED COMMUNICATION

On Day 28 you'll take your informal experiment a step further by exploring the possibility of communicating with distant individuals during the OBE. We recommend that you set up the session exactly as you did on Day 27, asking your friend to replace the first set of objects with a new and equally interesting collection. This time, however, you should ask your friend to remain in the location that will serve as the focus of your experiment for at least an hour. During this period, your friend should quietly relax, with eyes opened, in the chosen environment and passively notice any unusual thoughts, impressions, feelings, or images, carefully recording the exact time they occurred.

You, on the other hand, should select a ten-to-fifteen-minute time slot within the prearranged hour-long period. During this time slot, enter a state of alert relaxation and mentally "visit" your friend. As before, pay attention to any impressions of the objects your friend has chosen for this exercise. At the same time, devote some attention to "communicating with" or even "touching" your distant friend.

After you have completed your experience, record your impressions of the distant objects. Also record any mental "interaction" you may have attempted with your distant friend. Then, after the hour has ended, you and your friend should get back together and compare notes. Did your friend report a sense of tension during your mental "visit"? Did he or she notice anything unusual during the exact time you had your OBE? Did your friend sense your "presence" at all?

If you have your friend's permission, you may also wish to conduct a more spontaneous experiment. Instead of prearranging a particular time and place for the two of you to work together, you may spontaneously "visit" your friend *anytime* you have an OBE. The two of you can then compare notes.

It is easy to come up with variations on these informal experiments. You can work with cooperative pets, for instance, or with several friends instead of just one. You may also decide to use a variety of unusual materials and sensory impressions as additional focal points during these sessions. We expect that you'll come up with many fascinating variations on the informal experiments suggested here, and we wish you luck. In the meantime, some congratulations are in order. You've just completed Week Four of the Free Flight Program!

WEEK FOUR ROUNDUP Flying

DAY 22 THE NIGHT WATCH		DAY 23 THE MORNING AFTER	
Before you get out of bed, envision your face looking back at you from above. Then imagine yourself floating in the air above your body. After about twenty minutes, open your eyes and get up. Go about your day. During the time you would normally be going to sleep, watch a movie, listen to music, or read a book.	As the night wears on, observe your surroundings. Open your window and imagine yourself merging with the night. Close the window and continue to sit quietly while remaining awake. Toward morning, open the window and watch the sunrise. Observe other signs of life.	If you are particularly exhausted come morning, go to bed after telling yourself you may now have an OBE. If you still have some energy left, fix yourself a light-breakfast and take a walk for fifteen or twenty minutes. Return home, put on some music, and enter a state of alert relaxation. Picture your face looking back at you from above.	Remember your walk, and imagine that you are floating now along the route you took. Reaffirm your willingness to have an OBE and drift off to sleep. *(continued)*

WEEK FOUR ROUNDUP Flying (continued)

DAY 24 ORGASMIC FLIGHTS		**DAY 25** TIME TRAVEL	
Before you get out of bed, envision your face looking back at you from above. Then open your eyes and get up. Reflect on your own sexuality, focusing on the sensation of orgasm. Have an orgasm. Have another orgasm later in the day. Think about the orgasms you had, then let some time pass.	Conjure images of outer space, and come to orgasm while these images float through your mind. While on the verge of falling asleep, give yourself permission to have an OBE. Then see your face floating above you, and fall asleep.	Before you get out of bed, envision your face looking back at you from above. Then open your eyes and get up. Enter a state of alert relaxation. Focus your thoughts on a time and place in the distant past. As you concentrate, summon up as much detail as possible. Imagine the present time and place fading as the scene you are envisioning comes to the fore.	Sustain this mental sojourn for twenty or thirty minutes. Then, still in a state of alert relaxation, picture the scene of the distant past fading into a scene from the future. Maintain the future focus for twenty or thirty minutes. Resume a state of alert waking consciousness and continue your day.

		DAY 26 METAMORPHOSIS		
	While on the verge of falling asleep, give yourself permission to have an OBE. Then see your face floating above you, and fall asleep.	Before you get out of bed, envision your face looking back at you from above. Then open your eyes and get up. Sometime during the day, visit a zoo or aquarium, and find an animal you can identify with. Focus on that animal for twenty or thirty minutes. Mentally switch places with the animal. Distance yourself from the animal.	Return home, or find a comfortable nearby location, and enter a state of alert relaxation. As instructed on page 79, imagine yourself taking the form of your animal. In the animal form, look up and imagine a bubble. Imagine yourself merging with the bubble and observing the scene below. Imagine the bubble floating in the air above your own, human body.	Imagine the bubble merging with your body. Return to a state of alert waking consciousness. While on the verge of falling asleep, give yourself permission to have an OBE. Then see your face floating above you, and fall asleep. *(continued)*

WEEK FOUR ROUNDUP Flying (continued)

DAY 27 EXTENDED PERCEPTION		**DAY 28** EXTENDED COMMUNICATION	
Before you get out of bed, envision your face looking back at you from above. Then open your eyes and get up. Ask a friend to select a group of objects you've never seen before and place them in a familiar location. Enter a state of alert relaxation. Imagine the room around you dissolving as you mentally "visit" the objects.	"Observe" the objects for ten or fifteen minutes, then return to a state of alert waking consciousness. Make detailed notes of your impressions, then go to the location and compare your notes with what is actually there. While on the verge of falling asleep, give yourself permission to have an OBE. Then see your face floating above you, and fall asleep.	Before you get out of bed, envision your face looking back at you from above. Then open your eyes and get up. Ask your friend to replace the first set of objects with a second set. Also ask your friend to remain with the objects for the next hour. Enter a state of alert relaxation. Imagine the room around you dissolving as you mentally visit the objects and your friend.	During a ten-to-fifteen-minute time slot, "observe" the objects and even try to "communicate" with your friend. Then return to a state of alert waking consciousness. Make detailed notes of your mental activities and impressions, then go to the location and compare your notes with the actual objects and impressions reported by your friend.

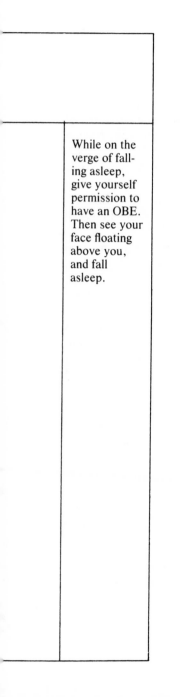

	While on the verge of falling asleep, give yourself permission to have an OBE. Then see your face floating above you, and fall asleep.

DAYS 29 AND 30

FREE FLIGHT

The Free Flight Program has taught you the basic skills required for exploring your inner capabilities and for inducing and enjoying OBEs. Exactly how you develop these skills in the future is entirely up to you. You may have found some of the exercises we've presented more suited to your personal capabilities, background, and interests than others. This is normal and can be expected, since different people are likely to respond to the various exercises in different ways. Now that you've studied all the exercises, we strongly encourage you to develop your own ongoing Free Flight Program by using and even refining those techniques that work best for you.

We recommend that you begin Day 29 with the early morning exercises you learned earlier in the Free Flight Program. Just as you feel yourself beginning to come out of deep sleep, and before you open your eyes or begin moving, concentrate on seeing the image of your own face looking back at you. Then focus on some distant place that you're interested in "visiting." After you begin to feel as if you're actually present in that distant environment, give yourself time to explore. If you are focusing on some recognizable location, do your best to notice any potentially verifiable information. After you feel satisfied with your experience, enter a state of full waking consciousness, and go about your day's activities.

Throughout the rest of the day affirm to yourself, whenever the thought occurs to you, that you are willing to have an out-of-body experience at some point in the future. Then let the thought go.

If you want, you may even spend part of your evening connecting with a special friend on a deeply personal, and possibly sexual, level. Incorporate into this mutual experience any of the basic interpersonal or sexual Free Flight exercises that seem appropriate. If you have the energy, complete this experience with a visit to a Jacuzzi or warm bathtub, bringing a friend along to watch over you. Relax in the warm rushing water as conducive music plays in the background. Allow yourself to take a mental journey alone or focus on inducing a shared OBE with a friend.

In the evening, as you're drifting off to sleep, once again affirm your openness to having an out-of-body experience. Then, as you feel yourself slipping into deep relaxation, focus your attention on some interesting place you would like to mentally "visit" either on your own or in cooperation with your friend.

Repeat the entire series of exercises on Day 30, including any variations you yourself have developed based upon your four weeks of firsthand experience in the Free Flight Program. Then take a few days off and enjoy the everyday world around you. It's time to celebrate! You've just opened your mind to a whole new dimension of inner experience, and graduated from the Free Flight Program.

APPENDIX A

A SPECIAL NOTE TO THE PHYSICALLY DISABLED

For the sake of simplicity, Free Flight instructions are written for those with no special disabilities. However, individuals with physical disabilities can tap the Free Flight techniques as well. In fact, in our work at the Institute for Advanced Psychology disabled individuals have helped us better understand a wide range of extended human capabilities. We therefore request that our disabled readers bear with us, and that they feel free to adapt the various Free Flight exercises to their personal requirements and capabilities.

In the first exercise, for example, readers are asked to explore their bodies by looking in the mirror. If you are blind, you can use a more tactile approach instead. In yet another exercise, readers are asked to explore the environment after temporarily blocking off vision. Those who are blind can alter their perceptions of the environment by blocking off their hearing instead.

The hearing-impaired may adjust the Free Flight exercises as well. For instance, when we ask you to focus on the sound of your own breathing, substitute the *feelings* associated with breathing for the sound. In the same fashion, you may substitute other sensory impressions for sounds throughout the thirty-day program.

If you are usually in a wheelchair or are otherwise restricted in your ability to move about, you can likewise adjust the program. Instead of walking around outside, for instance, you may simply visit another section of your home.

One last piece of advice: always feel free to skip a particular exercise, simply replacing it with one more suited to your requirements. It is also acceptable to proceed at the pace most comfortable for you and your individual situation.

We sincerely thank you for your interest and participation in the Free Flight Program. We hope it will help add a new dimension of enriching inner experience to your life.

—Keith Harary and Pamela Weintraub

APPENDIX B

•

FURTHER READING

Crookall, Robert. *The Interpretation of Cosmic and Mystical Experiences*. London: James Clark, 1969.

Crookall, Robert. *Casebook of Astral Projection*. New Hyde Park, N.Y.: University Books, 1972.

Fox, Oliver. *Astral Projection*. New Hyde Park, N.Y.: University Books, 1962.

Green, Cecilia. *Out of the Body Experiences*. London: Hamish Hamilton, 1968.

Mitchell, Janet Lee. *Out-of-Body Experiences: A Handbook*. New York: Ballantine Books, 1981.

Monroe, Robert. *Journeys Out of the Body*. Garden City, N.Y.: Doubleday, 1970.

Rogo, D. Scott. *Leaving the Body: A Complete Guide to Astral Projection*. New York: Prentice Hall Press, 1983.

Swann, Ingo. *To Kiss Earth Goodbye*. New York: Dell, 1975.

Acknowledgments

We wish to express our sincere gratitude to our spouses, Darlene Moore, who had the courage to close her eyes in Paris and open ours in California, and Mark Teich, who bore with the long nights of work.

We would also like to thank our colleagues and special friends who made a meaningful difference in helping us to explore the scientific, clinical, and personal dimensions of out-of-body experiences. This group most notably includes Dr. George Kokoris, Jerry Levin, Dr. John Hartwell, D. Scott Rogo, D. Celeste Ewers, Dr. Winston Cope, Dr. Diana Reiss, Patricia Walker, Dr. Harold Puthoff, and Anne Goldberg. To all those who have supported and encouraged our efforts but are not specifically mentioned here, please also accept our appreciation.

Special thanks also goes to our insightful and talented editor, Robert Weil, who came up with the thirty-day concept and encouraged and cajoled us through our work on this project. We would also like to express gratitude to Bill Thomas and Julia Pastore of St. Martin's Press, who helped to make our book publishing experience an extremely pleasant one. Very special thanks go to our literary agents, Roslyn Targ and Wendy Lipkind, who championed this volume and helped us publish it in numerous editions around the world.

We also extend our appreciation to our colleagues at Duke University and Duke University Medical Center who generously provided their advice, laboratory space, and equipment for much of the experimental research we have drawn upon in designing the Free Flight Program; to the Duke University administration for providing additional space on campus for our independent research; and to the American Society for Psychical Research, the Psychical Research Foundation, the Parapsychology Foundation, and the board of directors and board of scientific advisors of the Institute for Advanced Psychology for their role in furthering OBE and other advanced psychological research.

Last, but not least, we thank our two very special friends, Spirit and Soul, the hardworking cats whose patience and sensitivity made the original human-animal OBE communication/perception experiments a reality.

—Keith Harary and Pamela Weintraub

About the Authors

Keith Harary, Ph.D.,
has spent decades investigating the issues confronting those who are coping with extraordinary experiences. He is well known for the groundbreaking studies of out-of-body experiences conducted on the campus of Duke University in the early seventies. His research has included extensive laboratory and field research on the physiological and other variables associated with altered states of consciousness, including the development of specialized methods for actively inducing out-of-body experiences and other altered states.

Harary holds a Ph.D. in psychology, with emphases in both clinical counseling and experimental psychology. He has authored or co-authored hundreds of articles and eight books on topics related to perception, altered states of consciousness, personality, and related topics. He is currently Research Director of the Institute for Advanced Psychology in Tiburon, California, where he continues to conduct research in perception and other areas in association with an interdisciplinary consortium of scientists.

Pamela Weintraub
is a longtime magazine journalist living in New York City and the author of thirteen books. She was formerly the editor-in-chief of *Omni.*